MONOGRAPHS OF THE
SOCIETY FOR RESEARCH IN
CHILD DEVELOPMENT

Serial No. 243, Vol. 60, No. 1, 1995

YOUNG CHILDREN'S
KNOWLEDGE ABOUT THINKING

John H. Flavell
Frances L. Green
Eleanor R. Flavell

WITH COMMENTARY BY
Paul L. Harris
Janet Wilde Astington

MONOGRAPHS OF THE SOCIETY FOR RESEARCH IN CHILD DEVELOPMENT
Serial No. 243, Vol. 60, No. 1, 1995

CONTENTS

ABSTRACT

FLAVELL, JOHN H.; GREEN, FRANCES L.; and FLAVELL, ELEANOR R. Young Children's Knowledge about Thinking. With Commentary by PAUL L. HARRIS and JANET WILDE ASTINGTON. *Monographs of the Society for Research in Child Development*, 1995, **60**(1, Serial No. 243).

The 14 studies reported in this *Monograph*, taken together with previous research, suggest some important things that preschoolers (3–5-year-olds) do and do not know about *thinking*, broadly and minimally defined as mentally attending to something. They appear to know that thinking is an internal, mental activity that can refer to either real or imaginary objects or events. They are able to distinguish it from seeing, talking, touching, and knowing. They are sometimes able to infer that another person is thinking if given very clear and strong behavioral or situational cues: for example, when the person has been given a problem and looks reflective.

Generally, however, preschoolers are poor at determining both *when* a person (self or other) is thinking and *what* the person is and is not thinking about. They do not realize that people are experiencing a constant flow of ideation—William James's "stream of consciousness"—even when behaviorally and perceptually unengaged with the external world. They do not automatically assume the presence of mental activity even in a person who is so engaged—for example, when the person is looking, listening, reading, or talking. When they do assert that a person is thinking, they tend to be poor at inferring the content of the person's thought, even when the clues to its content are very clear and compelling. They are similarly poor at recognizing that they themselves have just been thinking and at recalling or reconstructing what they have been thinking about, even in situations designed to make accurate introspection very easy. These shortcomings are considerably less evident in 7–8-year-olds. These results suggest that preschoolers may regard thoughts as isolated, mysterious mental events, not linked to preceding causes or subsequent effects. The *Monograph* concludes with speculations about possible implications of their limited understanding of thinking and about factors that might influence the development of this understanding.

I. INTRODUCTION

A developmental psychologist shows a 5-year-old a candy box and asks her what is in it. "Candy," she says. She then looks inside the box and to her surprise discovers that it actually contains pencils, not candy. What would another child who had not yet opened the box think was in it? the experimenter now asks. "Candy!" says the child, amused at the trick. The experimenter then tries the same procedure with a 3-year-old. The response to the first question is the expected "candy," but the response to the second is surprising: "pencils." Even more surprising, the child also maintains that he himself had initially thought that pencils would be in the box. Unlike the 5-year-old, the 3-year-old shows no evidence of understanding that either he or other people could hold a belief that is false.

Results such as this are found in a new and exciting research area concerning the development of our knowledge and beliefs about the mental world—our folk psychology or naive theory of mind. More than did earlier metacognitive and social-cognitive investigations in the same domain, this new approach probes children's conceptions of the most fundamental components of the mind, such as beliefs and desires, and children's knowledge of how these components affect and are affected by perceptual inputs and behavioral outputs. In just a few short years, this fast-growing area has spawned scores of research articles and a number of book- and monograph-length treatments (see, e.g., Astington, 1993; Moses & Chandler, 1992; Perner, 1991; Wellman, 1990; Wellman & Gelman, 1992). Indeed, the spate of papers and posters on this topic at the 1993 meeting of the Society for Research in Child Development reminded several older participants of the way Piagetian research dominated the program in years past. Developmental findings in this area have also become of interest recently to a number of philosophers of mind, who believe that these findings may help clarify philosophical disputes about the nature of folk psychology—for example, whether it actually constitutes a folk *theory* (Ramsey, 1993).

The following are what we believe to be some of the highlights of theory-of-mind development, based on the research evidence to date (Flavell, 1993). The reader is cautioned that not all researchers would agree with all parts of our summary; there is considerable controversy in this area, much of it concerning the supposed acquisition of a mental-representational conception of the mind during the preschool period.

During infancy, children come to view people very differently from other objects. They see people as *compliant agents*, that is, as kindred creatures who move under their own power (agency) and are responsive to the infants' requests and other communications (compliance). Infants also acquire some sense of intentionality, recognizing that, unlike the behavior of objects, people's behavior makes reference to or is "about" something other than itself. Children demonstrate some capacity for empathy by the end of infancy, suggesting that by this point they have begun to construe people as experiencers as well as agents.

During the early preschool years, children acquire the basic distinction between mental and physical events. For instance, under some circumstances, they can distinguish between an imaged or imagined dog and a real dog. They show a beginning understanding of percepts, desires, emotions, and their interrelations. Thus, they know that another person viewing from a different position may not be able to see an object that they presently see. Also, they recognize that people are likely to feel sad or happy depending on whether their desires are fulfilled. Young preschoolers also develop pretense skills and the ability to interpret as pretense the make-believe of other people.

Later in the preschool period, according to some but not all experts in this area, children seem to acquire a rudimentary mental-representational conception of the mind. That is, they begin to sense that people form and act on mental representations of reality, representations that may not portray reality correctly. This newly acquired conception makes it possible for them to understand false beliefs, as in the foregoing candy-pencils task. Similarly, it enables them to think of deceptive or illusory objects and situations as appearing or seeming to be one thing to a perceiver while simultaneously really being something different. For example, older preschoolers readily understand that a straight object viewed through a distorting lens looks bent (i.e., is perceptually represented as being bent) but is really straight.

Subsequent to the preschool years, children further elaborate their understanding of minds as mental-representational devices. For example, they are increasingly aware that how people represent what they perceive will be influenced by the nature and quality of the perceptual information they receive and by their prior knowledge and experience. In addition, school age children endow themselves and other people with enduring personality traits, come to understand second- as well as first-order beliefs (i.e., beliefs about beliefs), and show numerous metacognitive acquisitions, such as knowledge about memory and memory strategies.

Most of the research in this area has focused on young children's understanding of mental *states*, such as beliefs, knowledge, desires, emotions, and intentions. For example, there have been numerous studies dealing with young children's developing understanding of desires and beliefs. In contrast, there has been little investigation of their knowledge about mental *activities*, that is, mental things that we could be said to *do* rather than just *have* (D'Andrade, 1987). The paradigmatic mental activity is that of *thinking*. Although as it progresses an act of thinking can become very complex, involving a complicated sequence of different processes such as inferring, comparing, judging, etc., it always begins with the minimal step of simply bringing something to mind or having something come to mind—thus, with taking some content as an object of thought, consciousness, or attention. That is, the necessary first step in thinking *about* anything is to think *of* it, that is, have it come to mind as an object of thought or mental attention. Indeed, one could argue that *thinking of* in this sense is our cognitive system's most basic and general activity.

What do young children know about thinking or mental attention, taken in this broad, minimal, and unelaborated sense of the mind just making some kind of mental contact with some content? There is surprisingly little direct evidence on the matter, given the importance and ubiquity of this activity. Piaget believed that, until well into the elementary school years, children fail even to make a clear ontological distinction between the mental and the physical (Piaget, 1929; see also Broughton, 1978; and Laurendeau & Pinard, 1962). As a consequence, younger children were said often to attribute physical properties to mental entities, a tendency to which Piaget referred as *childhood realism*. For instance, according to Piaget, they believe that thinking is talking, a physical activity, and that it is done with the mouth; similarly, they were said to believe that dreams are external, physical events that are potentially visible to others as well as to the dreamer.

However, subsequent research by Wellman and his colleagues (Estes, Wellman, & Woolley, 1989; Wellman, 1990, chap. 2; Wellman & Estes, 1986; Woolley & Wellman, 1992, 1993) convincingly showed that Piaget's testing procedures severely underestimated children's understanding of the mental-physical distinction. Using more sensitive measures than Piaget did, these investigators found that even 3-year-olds are capable of distinguishing between physical and mental entities, at least under some circumstances. For example, they realize that, whereas a real dog is a physical, public, tangible entity, an imaged or thought-of or dreamed-of dog has none of these properties. Indeed, 3-year-olds even distinguish mental entities from what Wellman and his colleagues refer to as *close impostors*, that is, invisible or intangible physical entities such as smoke and sounds that children might confuse with mental entities.

In addition, Johnson and Wellman (1982) found that by 4–5 years of age children tend to believe that a person needs a brain to think and also that the brain is located inside the head. This suggests that they may also construe thinking as an internal activity. Similarly, we (Flavell, Green, & Flavell, 1990) and Perner (1991) have argued on theoretical grounds that, although 3-year-olds generally do not understand the notion of *thinking that* (i.e., beliefs) because an understanding of beliefs requires a representational conception of the mind that most 3-year-olds have not yet acquired, they might understand something of the notion of *thinking of*, which does not require this conception. For example, Flavell et al. (1990) proposed that they understand that a person can be "cognitively connected" to an external object or event in various ways, for example, see it, hear it, and—probably— think of it. However, neither we (Flavell et al., 1990) nor Perner (1991) actually tested young children's understanding of thinking experimentally.

In this *Monograph*, we report a series of studies of young children's understanding of thinking or mental attention, as defined above. Chapter II presents six studies designed to find out whether they distinguish between thinking and four other object-directed activities or states with which they might be liable to confuse it: seeing, talking about, touching, and knowing. The four studies detailed in Chapter III investigated the situations in which

TABLE 1

Summary of Studies Reported in This *Monograph*

Chapter	Study	Ages of Subjects	Topic
II	1	3, 4	Differentiation of thinking from looking at and doing
	2	3	Differentiation of thinking from seeing
	3	3, 4	Differentiation of thinking from seeing, talking, and touching
	4	4, 5	Differentiation of thinking from knowing
	5	4	Differentiation of thinking from knowing
	6	4	Differentiation of thinking from knowing
III	7	4, 5, 7	Attribution of thinking in a variety of situations
	8	4	Attribution of thinking while problem solving, perceiving, and waiting
	9	3, 4, 5	Attribution of thinking and identification of what E is and is not thinking about
	10	4, 5	Attribution of thinking and identification of what E is and is not thinking about
IV	11	5	Introspection ability: very recent thinking
	12	5, 7–8	Introspection ability: very recent thinking
	13	5, 7–8	Introspection ability: very recent thinking
	14	5	Introspection ability: current thinking

young children do and do not attribute mental activity to other people and what they infer that the people are and are not thinking about when they do attribute it. Thus, the research reported in Chapter II explores what they think thinking is and is not, whereas that in Chapter III explores when they think people engage in it and what they infer its content to be. Chapter IV reports four studies of children's introspective ability, that is, their ability to detect and report the occurrence of mental activity in themselves rather than others. A great deal is known about the introspective abilities of adults (Ericsson & Simon, 1993; Farthing, 1992), but very little about those of young children. A brief summary of these 14 studies is provided in Table 1.

Finally, in Chapter V, on the basis of the results of these and other studies, we summarize what young children appear to know and not to know about mental activity. In that chapter, we also offer the following hypothesis as a possible explanation of these results: On the rare occasions when they think about ongoing mentation at all, young children tend to think of thoughts as isolated, largely inexplicable mental events, not linked to either prior causes or subsequent effects.

II. DIFFERENTIATION STUDIES

The six studies described in this chapter constituted our initial effort to determine what children know about the activity of thinking. Our research strategy was similar to the "close impostors" strategy of Wellman and his colleagues cited in Chapter I (Wellman, 1990). That is, we tried to see if young children distinguish the activity of thinking from four other psychological activities or states that it often accompanies and with which it therefore might be confused: knowing, acting, talking, and seeing. Three of the distinctive and essential characteristics of thinking become evident when we contrast it with these four. In contrast to knowing something, thinking of or about something tends to be an episodic, on-and-off activity rather than a continuous, enduring state (memory problems aside). Unlike physical action and talking aloud, thinking is covert. And, unlike seeing, it can and often does proceed in the absence of sensory input. Thus, one can think of something about which one has virtually no knowledge, and one can do so without seeing it, talking about it, or touching it. Conversely, one can know something without presently thinking about it, and one can see, talk, and act with relatively little thought or attention given to the objects or referents of these activities.

In Studies 1–3 we attempted to test young children's knowledge that a person could be thinking about something without seeing it, talking about it, or touching it. In Studies 4–6 we tried to find out whether they realize that a person could be thinking about something without knowing much about it and, especially, could know something without thinking about it at a given moment. Thus, our research strategy was to probe young children's beginning knowledge about thinking, not by asking them to describe thinking (difficult enough for adults, next to impossible for young children), but by finding out what they know it is not, as evidenced by what they distinguish it from. If they know that thinking (broadly and minimally defined as "mental attention to") is different from seeing, talking, physically acting, and knowing, then it is plausible to believe that they have at least some elementary understanding of it.

STUDY 1

The purpose of this preliminary study was simply to find out how easily young children could learn (with the experimenter's help) to distinguish what a depicted child was thinking about (portrayed in a "thought bubble") from what that child was looking at or doing.

Method

Subjects

Three groups of children were tested, with eight girls and eight boys in each group. The mean ages for the three groups were 3-3 (range 2-11 to 3-6), 3-10 (range 3-7 to 3-11), and 4-8 (range 4-6 to 5-0). The children in this and the other studies reported in this chapter attended a university preschool and were mostly from upper-middle-class backgrounds. Two female experimenters tested all the subjects in these studies. No child participated in more than one of Studies 1–3; similarly, no child participated in more than one of Studies 4–6.

Procedure

The experimenter began by modeling thinking for the subjects. She gave the topic of what she would think about, namely, her bedroom, and then described some of its contents. The subject was encouraged to do the same. The task stimuli were six drawings of children. In each drawing a child was shown doing one thing (e.g., looking at her mother, riding a bicycle) while thinking about something else (e.g., her teddy bear, kicking a football), which was illustrated in a thought bubble over the character's head. Two of the six pictures were used in pretraining to explain the idea of thought bubbles. The first showed a girl sweeping a floor, with a horse in the thought bubble over her head. The experimenter said, "Here is a girl named Jane. She is doing something. She is sweeping the floor. She is also thinking about something. This little picture shows us what she is thinking about." The experimenter pointed to the picture. "What is she thinking about? That's right, she is thinking about a horse. Is she thinking about a cat too? That's right/Actually she's not thinking about a cat because there's no cat in the picture. She's just thinking about that horse." We included this item to help the child understand that the character was thinking only of the object shown in the bubble. The same procedure was used with a second picture of a boy watching television and his thought bubble showing a hand cutting a cake.

Four test pictures were presented. In two of the pictures, characters were depicted as looking at one object while thinking of another. In one, for example, a girl was shown looking at her mother while thinking about her teddy bear. "Here's Sally and her mom. Sally is really *doing* something right now. Is she really looking at her mom? Sally is *thinking* about something right now. Is she thinking about her mom?" These questions were asked about the perceived object. In the other picture depicting looking at, the questions were asked about the object in the thought bubble. Thus, the yes-no questions were framed so that within each block the correct answer to one think question was "yes" and to the other "no." In the other two pictures, the depicted children were more actively engaged in physical activities; for example, a boy is riding a bicycle while his thought bubble depicts a foot kicking a football. The two types of items were blocked and counterbalanced over trials. Test questions were counterbalanced, with half the children receiving think before activity questions and half the reverse.

Results and Discussion

Table 2 shows the number of children in each age group performing perfectly on various numbers of the four tasks, that is, correctly answering both a task's thinking question and its doing question. Percentages of pairs of questions correctly answered were 72%, 81%, and 91% for the age 3, 3½, and 4½ groups, respectively—considerably higher than the 25% that would have been expected had the children responded randomly. The corresponding percentages for the think questions alone were 84%, 95%, and 100% (vs. 50% chance expectancy). Three (age) × 2 (sex) × 4 (task) mixed analyses of variance yielded no significant effects for the pairs scores, but they did reveal a significant age effect for think scores alone ($F[2, 42] = 3.98, p < .05$).

These data obviously cannot tell us exactly what the subjects thought *thinking about* meant. However, they constitute at least suggestive evidence that even the young 3-year-olds took it to be an activity different from

TABLE 2

Numbers of Children per Age Group in Study
1 Correctly Answering Pairs of Questions

	Correct Pairs				
Age Group	4	3	2	1	0
3	5	8	0	2	1
3½	9	4	2	0	1
4½	11	4	1	0	0

looking and overt motor actions. They appeared to understand the experimenter's initial examples of thinking and to follow her brief explanation of the thought bubbles fairly well (although a number of the youngest subjects, especially, incorrectly said "yes" in the pretraining when asked if the child was also thinking about an object not shown in the thought bubble). They were then able to use that information to map thinking onto what was inside the bubbles and looking and acting onto what was outside them.

Had the expression *thinking about* and its mental referent been completely meaningless to them, they might well have responded randomly to the thinking questions, or answered all of them in the affirmative, or assumed that all the thinking questions referred to what the character was doing overtly, thus taking *thinking about* to mean any observable action. The data presented in Table 2 show that most of them did none of these things. For example, only three subjects (all young 3-year-olds) answered all the thinking questions affirmatively. Similarly, subjects were no likelier to err on thinking questions than on doing questions—in fact, slightly the reverse (23 doing errors, 13 thinking errors). Consistent with the results of this study, Hadwin and Perner (1991) and Yuill (1984) have also found that 3-year-olds seem able to understand that thought bubbles depict a character's mental states rather than external reality.

STUDY 2

Although consistent with Hadwin and Perner's (1991) and Yuill's (1984) findings, the foregoing results obviously could have overestimated young children's ability to distinguish between thinking and other activities. That is, it is possible that many of the subjects in that study responded correctly just by mindlessly learning the pictorial conventions they were taught. They may have simply learned to say, without any genuine understanding, that the depicted child is "thinking about" whatever is shown inside the thought bubble and "really doing" whatever is shown outside it. In Study 2, we tried to determine what young 3-year-olds could infer about thinking without such explicit help. The specific objective was to find out whether they could distinguish thinking from seeing, at least to the extent of knowing that a person can think about things that he or she cannot see at that moment. Woolley and Wellman (1993; see also Wellman, 1990) have shown that children of this age seem willing and able to "imagine" objects to be present that are actually not present or that may not even exist anywhere (e.g., a purple turtle). Their positive findings, plus the suggestive results of Study 1, led us to expect that even young 3-year-olds might be able to make this thinking-seeing distinction.

Method

Subjects

Twenty-four children, 12 boys and 12 girls, participated in this study. Their mean age was 3-2 (range 2-10 to 3-7). One additional subject failed to complete the procedure.

Procedure

Following brief pretraining, two instances each of three types of tasks were given to the children. Experimenter 1 (E1) asked the second experimenter (E2, Ellie) to don a blindfold so that she could not see and to cover her ears with her hands so that she could not hear. Subjects were then asked three questions for each task. The first two questions concerned whether E2 could see the stimulus for that task and whether she could perform a physical movement (such as kicking her feet). The correct answer to the movement question was always "yes," and the correct answer to the see question was always "no," thus giving each subject a chance to say both "yes" and "no" prior to the critical third test question. In one task type (Present Object), the third question concerned E2's ability to think about an object she had recently been shown. In a second task type (Absent Location), it concerned her ability to think about a familiar location not currently visible (such as the child's classroom). In a third task type (Sense Object), it concerned her ability, not to think about something, but rather to feel the sensation caused by an object coming in contact with her hand, for example, when scraping her hand with a hard sponge. We expected children to perform correctly on this third task. This would demonstrate that children who thought that E2 could not think when not able to see and hear at least understood that she was still sentient—not totally "shut down."

Pretraining.—As in Study 1, E1 first modeled thinking by describing the contents of her bedroom and asking the child to do the same. Next, the child was asked to think about a previously seen object that was no longer visible. E1 covered a small white plastic spoon with a cloth and said, "Now let's think about that spoon. What color is it? Is it a big one or a little one? OK. Good." Finally, we attempted to convey to the child the notion that E2 was capable of doing certain things even though she was not currently doing them since the test questions all asked about what she could do rather than what she was doing. E2 sat across from the child, and E1 said to the child, "Right now, she's not clapping her hands, is she? But *can* she clap her hands right now? That's right/Actually she *can* clap her hands right now. Can she wiggle her fingers right now? That's right/Actually she *can* wiggle her fingers right now." We did not exclude children from the study on the basis of poor performance on these warm-up trials. Three subjects erred on both tasks, while an additional six subjects erred on one of them.

E2 was next asked to put on the blindfold and then asked whether she could see. She responded "no" and was then asked to cover her ears. She was asked whether she could hear, and she did not reply. E1 then said, "So right now Ellie can't see anything, and she can't hear anything. Let's talk about what things she can do and cannot do while she's like that, with her eyes blindfolded and her ears covered."

Testing.—The procedure is illustrated using the Present Object task. E1 briefly raised the blindfold and showed E2 a small doll, saying, "Here's something." E2 nodded, the blindfold was replaced, and the doll was placed on the table in front of her. The subject was then asked the following questions: "Can Ellie see this doll right now?" "Can Ellie stand up right now?" and, "Can Ellie think about this doll right now?" Corrective feedback was given, if necessary, for the first two questions but not for the critical third question. Different physical movements were mentioned for the other five tasks (kick her feet, open her mouth, move her legs, wiggle her nose, and shake her head). The second stimulus for the Present Object tasks was a colorful tea tin. The locations queried on the Absent Location tasks were the school's parking lot and the child's classroom. The Sense Object tasks involved questions about E2's ability to feel the sponge, as previously described, and to feel a large roll of tape rolled with some pressure over her hand. Half the subjects always received "see" questions before "movement" questions and half the reverse. There were two blocks of tasks, each including one task of each type in counterbalanced orders. For any given child the tasks in the two blocks were in the same order.

Results and Discussion

As Table 3 shows, subjects were usually able to say that E2 could think about objects she could not presently see (the mean percentage of correct responses to think questions was 76%). The numbers of subjects answering four, three, two, one, and no think questions correctly were 13, four, four, one, and two, respectively. Subjects correctly said that she could not see the object right now but that she could think about it right now (both questions correctly answered) on 71% of the Present Object and Absent Location tasks. On tasks on which subjects answered both initial see and move questions correctly (67% of the total), they answered 87% of the ensuing think questions correctly. Some of the children seemed to interpret the "can she" in the questions as "is she," at least on some trials, despite our effort to clarify the distinction in the pretraining. For example, nine subjects incorrectly said that E2 could not clap her hands and/or wiggle her fingers during

TABLE 3

PERCENTAGE CORRECT RESPONSES TO
QUESTIONS IN STUDY 2

	TASK TYPE		
QUESTION	Present Object	Absent Location	Sense Object
Think	77	75	...
See	90	98	90
Move	71	73	71
Feel	...	...	88

NOTE.—All percentages are significantly ($p < .05$) higher than chance expectation of 50% by t test.

pretraining, and 18 erred similarly on at least one of the six move questions. It is more than possible, therefore, that correct answers to the think questions would have been even more frequent had the children always interpreted them correctly as referring to what she was able to do rather than to what she was actually doing at that moment.

Despite this apparent tendency to misinterpret the questions on occasion, the children generally responded differentially and accurately to the three questions of each task, correctly answering the see question in the negative and the other two questions in the affirmative. We conclude from this response pattern that these young 3-year-olds at least realized that thinking about is not the same activity as seeing, that it could bear on physically absent as well as present objects, and that it could proceed in the absence of visual and auditory input. Thus, the results of this study suggest that the findings in our Study 1 and in Woolley and Wellman (1992) did not overestimate young 3-year-olds' knowledge about thinking.

STUDY 3

In Study 2 we found that young 3-year-olds appear to understand that a person *can* think about something while not able to see it. In Study 3 we tested whether, given strong situational and behavioral cues, young 3- and 4-year-olds can infer that a person *is* thinking about something while neither seeing it, talking about it, nor touching it. The study was designed to answer two questions. First, prior to any mention of the term in the experimental session, how likely would children of these ages be to describe as *thinking* a pensive-looking adult who had just been given a problem to solve? Second, after the term had been introduced, how likely would they be to recognize that the adult was *thinking about* the problematic stimulus even though turned away from it and clearly not seeing it, talking (aloud) about it, or touching it? That is, how easily can they differentiate, in this sense, thought from perception, speech, and action? Speech was added to perception and action in part to test Piaget's (1929) claim that young children tend to believe that thinking is situated in the mouth and consists of talking.

Method

Subjects

We initially tested 24 young 3-year-olds, 12 girls and 12 boys. Their mean age was 3-0 (range 2-8 to 3-5). We subsequently added a small comparison group of young 4-year-olds: six boys and six girls, with a mean age of 4-3 (range 4-0 to 4-5).

Procedure

The main tasks in this study were of two types: (a) three Problem Solving tasks, in which Experimenter 2 (E2, Ellie) was asked to explain a seemingly impossible occurrence, such as the disappearance of colorful pictures in a "magic" book, and (b) three Choice tasks, in which she was asked to choose between a set of four similar stimuli, such as which of four books she wished to take home. After Experimenter 1 (E1) presented the stimuli to E2 (and incidentally to the child) and asked either a Choice or a Problem Solving question of E2, E2 did not immediately respond. Rather, she turned her profile to the subject and assumed a stereotypical "thinking" pose. The child was then asked one of three pairs of questions for each task type. One question in each pair always asked whether E2 is thinking about the stimulus. The other asked whether she sees it, is talking about it, or is touching it—a different one of these questions for each pair. The correct answers to the thinking questions for the six tasks were always "yes," and the correct answers to the other, behavior questions were always "no."

In addition, two pretests, one of each task type, were given immediately prior to testing. In the pretests, rather than asking a pair of questions of the child, E1 simply asked the following open-ended question while E2 was in her thinking pose: "What is Ellie *doing* right now?" The word *thinking* had not been mentioned by either experimenter when this question was asked.

Tasks were blocked by type, and the order of the blocks was counterbalanced. The order of specific tasks within types was also counterbalanced, and the same ordering of think-behavior pairs of questions occurred within each task type. Specific stimuli were randomly assigned to the counterbalanced orders. Half the subjects were always given the think questions before the behavior questions and half the reverse.

Pretraining.—Children were asked three pairs of questions, to be sure that they could easily state that E2 was or was not seeing, touching, or talking about an object and to give them experience saying both "yes" and "no" to questions about her current activities. For example, E2 picked up a crayon, and E1 asked the child, "Right now, is Ellie *touching* this crayon with her fingers? That's right/Actually she *is* touching the crayon." (After any error and the corrective feedback, E1 again asked the question. All children then responded correctly.) E2 placed the crayon on the table, and E1 asked the child, "How about now? Is Ellie *touching* the crayon now? That's right/Actually she's *not* touching the crayon right now." The pair of seeing questions were asked about a mug, and the pair of talking questions concerned a small doll.

Pretest.—For one pretest (Postcards), E2 (and the child) was shown four colorful postcards of animals, and she commented on each one. E1 then asked, "Well, Ellie, I want to send one of these to our friend Barbara. Which card should I send to Barbara, Ellie?" E2 said, "That's a hard question. Hmmm. Give me a minute." She turned away so that her profile was visible to the child and made stereotypical thinking gestures (chin resting on raised hand, head tilted to one side, with a puzzled expression on her face), and E1 asked the child, "What is Ellie *doing* right now?" This question was included to determine whether the child understood with no prompting at all that the problem input plus the thinking gestures meant that E2 was thinking. Then, either after the child's answer or after the child failed to respond in a reasonable amount of time, E1 asked E2 to indicate her choice, which she did.

For the other pretest (Money Box), a box from a magic store was shown to E2 (and the child). E1 said, "This is a box. There is no money in there. Look at this!" E1 closed the box and then reopened it, and E2 exclaimed, "There's money in there now!" E1 said, "What a funny box! How did the money get in here, Ellie?" E2 again said, "That's a hard question. Hmmm. Give me a minute," and turned away with the same stereotypical thinking pose. E1 then asked the child, "What is Ellie *doing* right now?" After the child's answer, E1 again asked E2 how the money got into the box, and E2 offered an explanation of sorts: "I don't know, but maybe it was hiding inside the box." The two pretests were given in counterbalanced orders.

Test.—Except for the questions asked the child, the procedure for the Choice tasks was exactly like that for the Postcards pretest, and the procedure for the Problem Solving tasks was exactly like that for the Money Box pretest. The three Choice tasks were choosing which of four boxes E1 should give to her mother, choosing which of four books to take home, and choosing one of four soft drinks. The three Problem Solving tasks were explaining how a large pear got into an ordinary bottle with a narrow neck, explaining what happened to colorful pictures that disappeared as E1 leafed through a book from a magic store, and explaining what happened to red and blue scarves as they appeared to turn green and yellow, another magic store item.

On each task, after the problem was posed to E2 and she had turned away, E1 asked two questions: (*a*) "Right now, is Ellie *thinking* about the *x*?"; (*b*) one of the three behavior questions, "Right now, does Ellie *see* the *x*?" "Right now, is Ellie *touching* the *x*?" or, "Right now, is Ellie *talking* about the *x*?"

The 3-year-olds were given the two pretest tasks first and then the six main tasks in two blocks, as just described. Because the main tasks seemed quite easy for the 3-year-olds, we administered only one block of three main tasks to the 4-year-olds.

Results and Discussion

Table 4 shows how the two groups performed on the initial, open-ended pretest questions and on the subsequent, two-choice test questions. Only four of the 24 3-year-olds correctly responded "thinking" on one or both pretest trials when asked what reflective-looking E2 was "doing." Of the remaining 20, six reported what she was or was not looking at, and the rest either said "nothing" (two) or "I don't know" (seven) or else gave no answer (five). In marked contrast, 11 of the 12 4-year-olds responded that she was "thinking" on one or both pretest trials (10 did so on both trials). This age difference is significant ($\chi^2[2] = 18.51$, $p < .001$).

As Table 4 also shows, however, the 3-year-olds performed almost as well as the 4-year-olds on the subsequent test trials, on which the word *thinking* was supplied by E1 and subjects had to judge only whether E2 was engaged in this activity. Of the 24 3-year-olds, 19 responded correctly to at least five of the six think questions, one got four correct, and four got none correct. As in Studies 1 and 2, young 3-year-olds seemed able to distinguish

TABLE 4

PERCENTAGE CORRECT RESPONSES TO QUESTIONS IN STUDY 3

	PRETEST: "THINKING"	TEST			
AGE GROUP		Think	See	Talk	Touch
3	13	79	96	94	100
4	88	94	100	100	100

NOTE.—All percentages for the test questions are significantly ($p < .05$) higher than chance expectation of 50% by *t* test.

thinking from other psychological activities that frequently accompany it—in this study, the activities of seeing, talking about, and touching the object thought about. Contrary to Piaget's (1929) claim, they showed no evidence of systematically confusing thought with speech. On 69% of the think-talk trials they correctly said both that E2 was thinking about the problem stimuli and that she was not talking about them.[1]

These findings parallel those of a recent study in our laboratory by Rosenkrantz (1991), in which 20 3-year-olds (mean age 3-5) were tested for their ability to infer thinking from expressive cues. A videotape showed two women seated at a table with crayons and paper. One was actually drawing at that moment, looking at her paper. The other was holding her crayon away from the paper and looking up pensively. After a minute or so, the videotape was paused so that the women's expressions were frozen. After it was established that both women were engaged in coloring activity, the child was asked, "Which one is thinking?" For half the subjects, one woman played the thinker; for the other half, the roles were reversed. The 3-year-olds performed very well on this task: 19 of the 20 correctly identified the pensive-looking woman as the one who was thinking. Baron-Cohen and Cross (1992) have also shown recently that children of 3½ and 4 years of age identify as "thinking" that individual of a pair whose eyes are oriented away from the viewer and in an upward direction.

That young 4-year-olds know something about what thinking means, at least in a problem-solving context, is hard to doubt, given our results. Not only do they easily distinguish thinking from other activities, but, unlike young 3-year-olds, they also spontaneously characterize portrayed instances of reflection as *thinking* prior to any mention of the term by the experimenter. The concept of thinking is probably not as spontaneously accessible for 3-year-olds as it is for 4-year-olds. Nevertheless, our data, together with those of Baron-Cohen and Cross (1992), Rosenkrantz (1991), and Woolley and Wellman (1992), suggest that 3-year-olds also possess the concept in some form.

It might be objected that the young children in our studies really have no idea at all what sort of activity *thinking* refers to and therefore never have any grounds for saying that E2 is not doing it. That is, they can verify perceptually that she is not seeing, talking about, or touching the target object, but they cannot verify that she is not doing the unknown-to-them

---

[1] From reading the interview protocols that Piaget (1929) cited, it seems possible that at least some of his child subjects might have meant that thinking is *covert* speech, not (or not only) talking aloud. We were therefore on the watch for any evidence that our subjects identified thinking with subvocal talking. For example, subjects might say that E2 was "talking to herself" or "talking inside her head" when asked whether she was talking about the problem materials. No subject ever said anything of this sort, however.

activity that E1 refers to as *thinking about* it. Alternatively, it might be argued that they take *thinking* to mean "doing nothing." The evidence that they understand thinking would be more persuasive, according to these arguments, if children of this age could also be shown to *deny* that another person was thinking on some task.

Although we have not shown that they can deny thinking in the present investigations, we have shown it in three other recent studies (Flavell, Green, & Flavell, 1993). The data from these studies show that preschoolers are very willing to deny that a motorically and perceptually inactive person is thinking when that person has been given no cognitive task and does not look obviously pensive. In one study, on two trials in which one of the experimenters sat quietly, facing a blank wall, "waiting," the mean percentages of subjects saying that her mind was "empty of thoughts and ideas" rather than having some were 87%, 57%, 30%, and 12% at ages 3, 4, 6–7, and young adulthood, respectively. In a subsequent study, more than half of a group of 4-year-olds even said that her mind was "not doing anything" while she waited. Similar findings were obtained in Study 8 of the present investigation (Chap. III).

As we shall argue in Chapter III, these results suggest that young children do not realize that people are constantly experiencing mental contents of one sort or another—William James's ever-flowing "stream of consciousness" (James, 1890, p. 239)—even when not deliberately thinking about anything. More to the present point, however, they clearly show that preschoolers do not mindlessly attribute thinking activity to other people regardless of circumstances and that they do not take it to mean "doing nothing." On the contrary, they tend to believe that an inactive person who has no stimulus to perceive and no problem to solve, and who therefore appears to be doing nothing, may *not* be doing any thinking.

There are also other reasons to doubt the plausibility of these objections. First, they obviously do not apply to the results of the Baron-Cohen and Cross (1992) and Rosenkrantz (1991) studies, in which the question to the subjects was which of two individuals was thinking (an ordinary two-choice question) rather than whether a single individual was thinking (a yes-no question). It seems most unlikely that 95% of Rosenkrantz's 3-year-olds would correctly identify the pensive-looking woman as the one who was thinking if they had no idea at all what *thinking* meant. Second, it does not even seem a plausible explanation of children's behavior in the present study. At the moment when the child is asked whether E2 is thinking about the problem stimuli, E2 has averted her gaze from the stimuli and does not appear to be doing anything that pertains to them at all. Had the children construed *thinking about x* to mean only "acting on *x* in some unknown way," they should have denied rather than affirmed that she was thinking about *x* at that moment because she appeared to be totally disconnected from *x* psychologically. Only if they had understood *thinking about* to refer to a mental activity requiring no physical orientation toward, or contact with, its object should they have found it natural to say, as they usually did say, that she was thinking about it. The same argument could be made for the Absent Location trials in Study 2, on which 3-year-olds usually said that E2 "could think about *x* right now" when *x* was a physically absent place (see also Woolley & Wellman, 1992).

STUDY 4

Studies 1–3 were designed to test preschoolers' ability to distinguish the activity of thinking about from those of seeing or looking, talking, and touching or other motor behaviors. In contrast, Studies 4–6 were designed to test their ability to distinguish the episodic activity of thinking from the continuous state of knowing. Knowing and thinking are both internal, quintessentially "mental" phenomena, and young children may not easily differentiate between them. We are aware of no previous studies of children's ability to distinguish them.

Thinking about *x* and knowing about *x* are often both present or both absent, of course. For example, I may know where my keys are and also be thinking about where they are at this moment. Conversely, I may not know where they are and also not be thinking right now about where they might be. However, the state and the activity can also be clearly distinguished; consequently, one can have either one without the other. For instance, I may not know where my keys are but be thinking about (wondering about, searching memory for) their possible whereabouts. Conversely, I may know exactly where they are but not happen to be thinking about their location at this moment. The latter is an especially common dissociation: there are obviously many things that people know that they seldom if ever think about.[2]

In Studies 4–5 we tested preschoolers' ability to identify instances of each of these four possibilities; the latter two, in which thinking and knowing have to be differentiated, were naturally of particular interest. Pilot work indicated that the tasks that we were able to design to test this ability were too complex to be appropriate for 3-year-olds. Consequently, the subjects tested in these investigations were 4-year-olds (Studies 4–6) and young 5-year-olds (Study 4).

---

[2] There are several other things to learn about knowing that we did not try to assess in Studies 4–6, e.g., that knowing implies a true belief (Montgomery, 1992).

Method

Subjects

Two groups of children were tested: 16 4-year-olds (seven girls and nine boys) with a mean age of 4-6 (range 4-2 to 4-11) and 16 young 5-year-olds (six girls and 10 boys) with a mean age of 5-2 (range 5-0 to 5-7). One additional subject was dropped because he was not proficient in English.

Procedure

Subjects were given six tasks: two Know–Not Think (K-NT) tasks, two Not Know–Think (NK-T) tasks, one Know-Think (K-T) task, and one Not Know–Not Think (NK-NT) task. Two experimenters alternated roles from task to task in searching for lost objects (E2) and asking the test questions (E1).

The subject was introduced to the study by E1 saying, "Today we are going to play a game where I will ask you some questions about *knowing* about things and about *thinking* about things." E2 then began to search for a lost object. The procedure is illustrated by a K-NT task. E2 said, "I put my good pen somewhere in this room. It's not in my purse. It's not on the table. You don't have it, do you [asked of E1 and the child]? Aha. It was under the table. I'll put it right here on the floor." E1 placed a new object in front of E2 and asked, "Hey [Francie], here's a funny bird to find out about." E2 said, "OK, I can do that. I found my pen." She then examined this distractor object as E1 asked, "Right now, is Francie *thinking* about this bird?" Next the child was asked two questions in counterbalanced order: "Right now, is Francie *thinking* about where her pen is?" and, "Does Francie *know* where her pen is?"

The other tasks were very similar, except for E2's response to E1's request that she find out about the distractor item. In the NK-NT trial, she agreed to examine the distractor item, saying, "OK, I can do that. I'm not going to find my scissors." In the K-T trial, she waved away the distractor item and stared hard at her backpack, where she had just located her checkbook, saying, "No, I can't do that. I've got to concentrate on where my checkbook is." In the NK-T trials, she refused, saying, "No, I can't do that. I've got to find my [keys]," and assumed the same stereotypical thinking pose used in Study 3. Thus, the function of the distractors was to suggest strongly to the children where E2's thinking was directed: toward the distractor and away from the target in the Not Think tasks and toward the target and away from the distractor in the Think tasks.

The tasks were divided into two blocks and the blocks counterbalanced across subjects. In one block, K-NT tasks appeared in the first and third positions and the K-T task second. In the other block, NK-T tasks appeared in the first and third positions and the NK-NT task second.

Results and Discussion

Table 5 shows how subjects in each age group performed on the Know questions and the Think (about the target object) questions on the four types of tasks. A 2 (age) × 2 (type of Know task: the three Know tasks vs. the three Not Know tasks) mixed analysis of variance was performed on children's answers to the Know questions. This analysis yielded as its only significant result a main effect for type of task ($F[1, 30] = 10.43, p < .01$). As Table 5 shows (see the four "Know" columns), this means that subjects were significantly better at saying correctly that E2 did not know where the target object was when she had in fact not found it (an average of 93% correct on the Know questions of the NK-T and NK-NT tasks) than they were at saying correctly that she did know where it was after she had found it (an average of 67% correct on the Know questions of the K-NT and K-T tasks). Perhaps not having succeeded in finding something is more salient or more certain evidence of not knowing where it is for young children than having found it is evidence for (subsequently) knowing where it is. Also, on the K-T task, E2's rather unnatural insistence on continuing to concentrate on her backpack, in which she had just found her checkbook, may have been taken by some children as an indication that she really did not know, or was no longer quite sure, where her checkbook was.

A similar analysis of variance was also carried out on children's answers to the Think questions. Again, the only significant finding was a main effect for type of task ($F[1, 30] = 19.95, p < .001$). In contrast to the pattern on the Know questions, the children were more accurate at identifying when

TABLE 5

PERCENTAGE CORRECT RESPONSES TO KNOW AND THINK
QUESTIONS IN STUDY 4

	TASK							
	K-NT		NK-T		K-T		NK-NT	
AGE	K	T	K	T	K	T	K	T
4	56	56	97*	94*	56	88*	94*	38
5	78*	41	88*	94*	75*	81*	94*	38

NOTE.—K = know, T = think, and N = not. Thus, K-NT means a task in which E2 knows where the target object is but is not thinking about where it is at that moment. Percentages significantly ($p < .05$) higher than chance expectation of 50% by t test are marked with an asterisk.

E2 was thinking about the target (an average of 91% correct on the Think questions of the NK-T and K-T tasks) than at identifying when she was not (44% correct on those of the K-NT and NK-NT tasks).

Again, we can only speculate that the evidence may have seemed more obvious or compelling to them in the former case than in the latter. On the Think trials she refused to look at the distractor object and talked and acted as though she were still thinking only about the target object. On the Not Think trials, however, the evidence that she was no longer thinking about the target object was more indirect and less conclusive. It consisted only of her turning her attention to the proffered distractor object. Perhaps some of the children believed, not unreasonably, that she might still be giving occasional thought to the whereabouts of the target while attending to the distractor. They might be especially likely to believe this when the target had not been found; consistent with this possibility, note the especially poor performance (38% correct) on the NK-NT task's Think question. It is also possible that they were readier than adults would have been to assume that E2 was thinking about both target and distractor at the same time because children of this age are less aware than adults are of limitations on attentional capacity (Pillow, 1988, 1989a). Whatever the reason, subjects did say that E2 was thinking about both the target and the distractor fairly often—on 39% of the trials.

Despite the puzzling unevenness of their performance over different tasks, the children gave little evidence of equating thinking and knowing—the question of principal interest. For example, on 76% of the tasks on which they should have given different answers to the Know and Think questions (i.e., the K-NT and NK-T tasks), they did give different answers. As Table 5 shows, they found it particularly easy to say that E2 was thinking about where the lost object might be but did not know where it was (NK-T tasks).

STUDY 5

This study had two objectives. The first was to find out whether 4-year-olds would be able to differentiate thinking and knowing more easily if the processing demands of the task were reduced. Accordingly, instead of asking subjects two Think questions and one Know question on each task, as in Study 4, the experimenter first supplied the answer to the two Think questions (target and distractor) and then asked only the Know question. The second objective was to find out whether children would understand knowledge questions better if they were worded more concretely. Perhaps children of this age understand what it means to know something as opposed to thinking about it but are not clear about the meaning of the word *know.* To test this possibility, half the subjects (Know group) were always asked whether the second experimenter "knows" where the target object is, as in Study 4, and the other half (Tell group) whether she "can tell us" where it is.

Method

Subjects

Two groups of 4-year-olds were tested: a Know group of nine girls and seven boys (mean age 4-5, range 4-0 to 4-11) and a Tell group of eight girls and eight boys (mean age 4-5, range 4-1 to 4-10).

Procedure

The procedure was identical to that of Study 4 except that subjects were explicitly told, rather than asked, the correct responses to the two Think questions and then were asked a single Know question, using either the "know" or the "tell" wording. For example, on the Know–Not Think (K-NT) pen task previously described, for half the subjects E1 said, "Right now, Francie is *thinking* about this bird. She is *not* thinking about where her pen is. Does Francie *know* where her pen is?" For the other half she said, "What if we ask her where her pen is? Can Francie tell us where it is?"

Results and Discussion

Table 6 shows how the subjects in the Know and Tell groups responded to the Know questions on the four types of tasks. The corresponding percentages from the Know questions of Study 4 are included for comparison

TABLE 6

PERCENTAGE CORRECT RESPONSES TO KNOW AND TELL
FORMS OF KNOW QUESTIONS IN STUDY 5

	TASK			
GROUP	K-NT	NK-T	K-T	NK-NT
Know	72*	94*	31	94*
	(56)	(97*)	(56)	(94*)
Tell	75*	84*	50	88*

NOTE.—For the meaning of K, T, and N, see Table 5. The figures in parentheses are the comparable percentages from Study 4 (see Table 5). Percentages significantly ($p < .05$) higher than chance expectation of 50% by t test are marked with an asterisk.

purposes. This comparison shows that the present study's reduction in processing requirements had no appreciable beneficial effect on children's performance.

A 2 (question form) × 2 (type of task: Know vs. Not Know) mixed analysis of variance yielded as its only significant result a main effect for type of task ($F[1, 30] = 8.03$, $p < .01$). This analysis confirms what is apparent from Table 6: the wording of the question had little influence on the children's answers. Their ability to identify whether the experimenter knew the target object's location was neither helped nor hurt by asking them if she could tell us where it was rather than simply asking them if she knew where it was. The similarity in the two patterns of responses suggests that in both cases the children had a fairly accurate understanding of what they were being asked (whether the experimenter knew/could report the whereabouts of the target object), whether or not they were able to answer correctly. As in Study 4, the children were significantly better at correctly diagnosing absence of knowledge than presence of knowledge. We do not know why and could only reiterate the speculations offered in the discussion of Study 4.

More important, however, is the fact that there is again little evidence to suggest that the children confused thinking with knowledge or construed them as the same mental phenomenon. Much as in Study 4, on 81% of the tasks on which they should have said that she knew where the object was when told that she was not thinking about it, or the reverse, they did so (the two leftmost data columns of Table 6). Similarly, the children's surprisingly frequent errors on the Know-Think (K-T) task, whatever their cause, also testify to a willingness to deny knowing-where even when thinking-about-where has just been affirmed by the experimenter.

STUDY 6

The purpose of Study 6 was to provide additional tests of 4-year-olds' ability to distinguish between thinking and knowing. In some of these tests the children themselves rather than the experimenter supplied the names of items that they thought the second experimenter would not be thinking about at that moment; the children were then asked whether the second experimenter knew about those items. Using not-thought-about items generated by the children themselves seemed a better test of their understanding than using ones provided by the experimenter. In addition, most of the knowledge in question concerned matters other than object location: it included not-further-specified "knowledge about" certain items and also factual knowledge that the second experimenter could be assumed to know (e.g., what her mother's name is).

Method

Subjects

Sixteen 4-year-olds (nine girls, seven boys) participated in this study. The mean age was 4-5 (range 4-0 to 4-11). One additional child was excluded because during the second part of the study she would never agree with the premise that E2 was not thinking about a given item.

Procedure

The children were first given brief practice in generating the names of articles of clothing that one of the experimenters was and was not wearing that day. The other experimenter then said, "In this game today I need your help deciding some other things about Francie. She's thinking about some things right now and *not* thinking about other things. She is getting ready to go on a picnic this weekend, and she is deciding what things she needs to take. She is making a list. What is Francie thinking about right now? That's right/Actually she's thinking about things she will take on her picnic, isn't she? There are some things she is probably *not* thinking about right now. Tell me something she is probably *not* thinking about right now." If the child was very slow to respond, E1 prompted by saying, "Francie is probably not thinking about. . . . Ummm. . . . Good. She's probably not thinking about [whatever the child said]. Anything else she's probably not thinking about? Good. She's probably not thinking about [whatever the child said]." E1 then asked about E2's knowledge of the things the child had suggested she was not thinking about: "OK. You said she is probably *not* thinking about *x* right now. Does she *know* about *x*?"

While E2 continued to write her picnic list, E1 introduced the first of three additional tasks, always given in fixed order. The tasks concerned E2's knowledge of her mother's name, the color of her car, and her age. The procedure is illustrated for the name task. E1 said, "My turn. Right now, she is *not* thinking about . . . ummm . . . her mother's name. Is she thinking about her mother's name right now? That's right, she is not thinking about her mother's name right now. Does she *know* what her mother's name is?" Following the three tasks, the child was given another opportunity to generate an item that E2 was probably not thinking about. E1 said, "Your turn. Can you think of other things Francie is probably *not* thinking about right now? Good. Does she *know* about [whatever the child said]?"

The session concluded with a brief probe to determine whether subjects would expect that a person engrossed in thinking about one thing would be likely to be also thinking about another, unrelated thing simultaneously, as children often did in Study 4. E2 said, "Has anybody seen my moose [a stuffed animal]? It used to be someplace in this room." E1 searched and found the moose and said, "Here he is. Over here in the box. I'll put him right back there so he'll be safe. Here's a book you might like to look at, Francie." E2 said, "OK, I would like to see this book," and she studied a complex picture. E1 said, "Right now, Francie is thinking about that book, isn't she?" For half the subjects, the first test question was then phrased, "Is she thinking about her moose?" For the other half of the subjects, the question was, "Is she thinking about her moose too?" The final question was, "Does she *know* where her moose is?"

Results and Discussion

Twelve of the 16 children were able to generate from one to three things that they said E2 was not thinking about while making her picnic list. The most frequent categories of items nominated were foods and animals. Of the 22 items nominated, 18 (82%) were accompanied by affirmative answers to the subsequent Know question, which we regarded as correct. For example, one child thought that E2 was not "thinking about" kiwis and pets but did "know about" both those things. For each of the familiar items that E1 said that E2 was not presently thinking of (her age, the color of her car, and her mother's name), 13 of the 16 subjects (81%) correctly asserted that E2 knew that fact; 12 of those 13 were correct on all three items. Immediately following the questions about these familiar items, subjects were asked if they could think of still other things that E2 was probably not thinking about at that moment. Eleven subjects proposed a total of 16 such items, with 11 (69%) of these accompanied by claims that E2 nevertheless knew about those items. In the final probe that followed, eight of the 16 children said that E2 was thinking about (or "still" thinking about) the stuffed animal that she had just found and had then put away, in addition to the book that she was currently looking at and about which E1 said she was now thinking; all 16 said that she knew where that animal was.

As in Studies 4 and 5, therefore, most of the children readily differentiated between thinking and knowing, usually asserting that E2 had knowledge of things about which she was not currently thinking. It is also possible that some of their assertions that she did not know about a given item were based on a sincere guess that she did not, rather than on a lack of understanding of what it means to know something. Similar to what was observed in Study 4, half the children also gave evidence of believing that E2 could and did think about two things at once, by claiming that she continued to think about a previously attended to but now abandoned object while also thinking about the current object of her attention. As we see in the next chapter, we tested for this belief more systematically in Study 10.

III. SITUATIONS STUDIES

The studies described in Chapter II, taken together with previous studies by others, suggest that by age 4 or thereabouts children have come to conceive of *thinking* (broadly defined) as an internal activity that is distinguishable from perception, talking, acting, and knowing. What else is there for them to learn about it? One of its most characteristic features is its tendency to flow incessantly—the continuous "stream of consciousness" that William James (1890, p. 239) and many others (e.g., Pope & Singer, 1978) have described.

There is some evidence that adults tend to believe, with James, that something thought-like is going on in the mind of a conscious person virtually all the time. An unpublished questionnaire study that we carried out recently with 234 college students showed that 76% thought that the following statement was "probably true," 12% thought that it was "probably not true," and 12% checked "no opinion": "Conscious mental events (ideas, percepts, images, feelings) normally follow one another more or less continuously in a person who is awake. They form a kind of 'stream of consciousness,' with first one conscious mental event happening, then another, then another." Similarly, in a subsequent experimental study (Flavell et al., 1993), briefly cited in Chapter II and to be described further presently, 95% of a group of college student subjects said that an experimenter who just sat quietly "waiting," with no perceptual or behavioral task to do, was nonetheless having "some thoughts and ideas."

The question arises as to whether young children also understand that mental activity goes on virtually all the time in a conscious individual. Study 3 (Chap. II) showed that 4-year-olds would readily say that a person who has been given a problem and who acts stereotypically reflective is "thinking"; that is, they seemed willing to attribute mental activity at least when situational and behavioral cues very strongly suggested its presence.

Flavell et al. (1993) tested their willingness to attribute it in other situations as well. In the first of three studies, 3-year-olds, 4-year-olds, 6–7-year-olds, and college students observed one of the experimenters in three situations: (a) two Wait trials, in which she just sat quietly, facing a blank wall; (b) a Looking trial, in which she looked at pictures; and (c) a Problem Solving trial, in which she had the task of trying to figure out how a large object had gotten inside a narrow-necked bottle. In each situation, subjects were asked to indicate, using empty and nonempty thought bubbles, whether the experimenter was "having some thoughts and ideas" or whether, instead, "her mind was empty of thoughts and ideas." Subjects had been given examples of these two mental states during pretraining: idle thoughts and ideas coming to the experimenter's mind one after another while on her way to school versus an empty mind while she was "deep asleep and not dreaming" the previous night.

The two older groups were likelier than the two younger ones to attribute some thoughts and ideas to the experimenter in the Looking situation (95% vs. 80%) and in the Problem Solving situation (100% vs. 65%). However, the age increase in attribution was much more pronounced in the case of the Wait trials. The percentages of 3-year-olds, 4-year-olds, 8-year-olds, and adults attributing some thoughts and ideas on both Waiting trials were 5%, 20%, 55%, and 95%, respectively.

The second and third studies (Flavell et al., 1993) used only 4-year-olds as subjects. In the second study, we strongly emphasized that "thoughts and ideas" should include idle, undirected ones as well as directed ones. Nevertheless, the mean percentage of correct Waiting trials was similar to that found in the first study for this age group. In addition, 62% of the children said that, if she tried, the experimenter would be able to keep her mind "completely empty of all thoughts and ideas" for 3 min (a period of time with which subjects had been familiarized just previously). In contrast, in the aforementioned unpublished questionnaire study, only 9% of 234 college students thought it "probably true" that "the average person can completely rid his or her mind of all conscious experiences for long periods of time." Finally, in the third study, 4-year-olds also tended to say that the mind of a waiting person was "not doing anything" rather than that it was "doing something."

The results of the three studies reported in Flavell et al. (1993) suggest that, unlike older children and adults, young children do not assume that mental activity goes on more or less continuously in a waking person, whether or not the situation or the person's appearance suggests its presence. The purpose of Studies 7 and 8 was to explore this possibility further.

STUDY 7

The purpose of this study was to find out how likely subjects of different ages would be to attribute mental activity to a person in a variety of different situations. After brief pretraining on the meaning of key terms, children and adults were shown pictures of child characters in nine different situations. In five of these, the activity in which the character was said to be engaged directly implied the presence of some mental activity: (1) listening; (2) looking; (3) reading; (4) talking; and (5) deciding. In the other four, there was no overt activity or task: the character was just sitting quietly, either (6) following a neutral, commonplace event, (7) following an emotionally negative event, (8) prior to an anticipated negative event, or (9) asleep and not dreaming. Subjects were asked to judge whether there was "anything going on in the character's mind" in each of these situations.

On the basis of the results obtained in Flavell et al. (1993), we expected that adults and children would show different patterns of responses to these situations. We thought that the adults would say that something was going on in the character's mind in all the situations, except perhaps situation 9. In contrast, we guessed that young children might be more likely to attribute mental activity in situations 1–5, in which the character's present behavior directly implied it, than in situations 6–8 (especially 6), in which it did not. We also thought that, because of the differences in affect, they would be more apt to attribute mental activity in situations 7–8 than in situation 6. We assumed that they would seldom attribute it in situation 9, which we viewed as a kind of baseline or control condition.

Method

Subjects

Three groups of children and one group of college students were tested, with 19 subjects in each group. The mean ages for the children were 4-6 (range 4-0 to 4-11), 5-6 (range 5-1 to 5-11), and 7-5 (range 6-5 to 8-2). The 4-year-old group, consisting of eight girls and 11 boys, was drawn from a university laboratory preschool. The 5-year-old group, composed of eight boys and 11 girls, came from two kindergarten classrooms in a private elementary school. The 7-year-old group, consisting of seven boys and 12 girls, was drawn from two private schools. Thirteen women and six men composed the college sample. All the subjects were from upper-middle-class backgrounds. No subject was excluded from the study. The same female experimenter tested each subject.

Procedure

The pretraining was as follows. The experimenter said, "Today we are going to talk about what goes on in people's minds. Like, do you know what is going on in my mind right now? Well, I'm *paying attention* to you, and I'm *thinking* that you are a nice girl/boy/person. Now I'm *thinking* about some pictures I'm going to show you, and I'm *feeling* happy because I like to talk to children/people. Is there something going on in *your* mind right now? Is there something you are *paying attention to* or *thinking about* or *feeling*? Maybe you are *wondering* in your mind about what we are going to be doing—that's one thing that might be going on in your mind right now. Or maybe there is something else that is on your mind right now. Is there? So I'll be showing you pictures of people and asking you whether you think there is anything going on in *their* minds or not. Maybe there will be, and maybe there won't be."

Only the back of each character's head was shown in each of the nine drawings. Further, if, for example, the character was said to be listening to a story about elephants, the book was not depicted. We did include and describe a distractor object in each picture that was not the current object of thought of the character. For example, a table holding an incomplete puzzle was positioned behind the person listening to the story. We reasoned that a subject not truly understanding the relation of current input to thought might false alarm to these distractor objects, saying incorrectly that the character was thinking about them.

We illustrate the procedure for the *Listen* task. The experimenter introduced the picture just described of a female sitting in a chair. The experimenter said, "Carol is listening to a story about elephants. There is a puzzle on the table behind her. While Carol is listening, do you think there is anything going on in her mind, or *not?*" If the subject said "yes," the experimenter then asked, "What might be going on in her mind?" The nine line drawings were presented in individually randomized orders. The wording for the remaining tasks was as follows:

> *Look.*—"Helen's brother drew a picture of a boat and gave it to Helen to look at. Helen is looking at the picture. There are some roller skates on the floor behind her. While Helen is looking, do you think anything is going on in her mind, or *not?*"
>
> *Read.*—"Cynthia's reading a book about insects. Her shoes are under her chair. While Cynthia is reading. . . ."
>
> *Talk.*—"George is talking to his mom about a birthday party he went to. His bird is in a cage behind him. While George is talking to his mom. . . ."
>
> *Decide.*—"Jim's dad gave him some money. Jim is trying to decide whether to buy a hotdog or an ice-cream cone. He is wearing a baseball cap. While Jim is deciding. . . ."
>
> *Neutral (sitting quietly after neutral event).*—"While Angel was eating breakfast she watched her mom wash the dishes. A little while later,

Angel is sitting quietly on the rug in her room all by herself. She is wearing a pink bow in her hair. While Angel is sitting there. . . ."

Past Negative (sitting quietly after negative event).—"When Larry woke up this morning, he discovered his hamster had gotten out of its cage and had run away. He couldn't find it anywhere. And his mother said they will probably never see it again. A little while later, Larry is sitting quietly in a chair all by himself. His skateboard is on the floor behind him. While Larry is sitting there. . . ."

Future Negative (sitting quietly before negative event).—"John has been sick. His mom is going to take him to the doctor to get a shot. He doesn't like shots. They are leaving in a little while. John is sitting on the side of his bed all by himself. His toy cars are under his bed. While John is sitting there. . . ."

Asleep (sleeping and not dreaming).—"Before Mary went to bed she put her clothes away. She was very tired when she went to sleep. She is so tired that she isn't even dreaming about anything. Her doll is on the bed next to her. While Mary is sleeping there and *not* dreaming. . . ."

Results and Discussion

Table 7 shows the percentages of subjects saying that there was something going on in the story characters' minds while they were in the various different situations. Shown in parentheses are the percentages of subjects who both said that something was going on in the character's mind and also went on to make an at least fairly plausible inference as to what it might be, in response to the experimenter's "What might be going on in her

TABLE 7

PERCENTAGE OF SUBJECTS ATTRIBUTING MENTAL ACTIVITY TO PEOPLE
IN VARIOUS SITUATIONS IN STUDY 7

	SITUATION								
AGE	Listen	Look	Read	Talk	Decide	Neutral	Past Neg.	Future Neg.	Asleep
4	58	53	53	74	63	47	68*	58	32
	(26)	(16)	(42)	(32)	(42)		(47)	(37)	
5	68	74	84*	79*	79*	79*	100*	89*	37
	(21)	(50)	(63)	(42)	(68)		(89)	(79)	
7	79*	63	84*	79*	84*	58	95*	95*	16*
	(68)	(42)	(74)	(58)	(84)		(95)	(84)	
Adult	100*	100*	100*	95*	100*	84*	100*	100*	37
	(95)	(95)	(100)	(89)	(100)		(95)	(100)	

NOTE.—Percentages significantly ($p < .05$) different from chance expectation of 50% by t test are marked with an asterisk. The figures in parentheses show the percentage of subjects giving plausible answers to the experimenter's follow-up question, "What might be going on in her mind?"

mind?" question. Inferences were judged plausible if they made at least minimal reference to the story character's psychological activity or situation: what or who the character was listening to, looking at, reading about, talking to or about, deciding about, or feeling sad or apprehensive about. A typical plausible inference would be to say that the character was "thinking about the birthday party" in the Talk situation ("thinking about" was the most commonly used expression at all age levels). Reference solely to the distractor objects, or to content unrelated to the situation, was not scored as a plausible inference; responses that included such references in addition to plausible content were scored as plausible inferences, however. Since plausibility could not be defined clearly in the case of the Neutral and Asleep conditions, it was not scored for those conditions.

A 4 (age group) × 2 (situation: the leftmost five situations in Table 7 vs. the next three) mixed analysis of variance was performed on subjects' "yes" responses to the initial mental activity attribution question. This analysis yielded as its only significant result a main effect for age ($F[3, 72] = 11.29, p < .001$). The percentages of "yes" responses across these eight tasks combined were 59%, 83%, 80%, and 97%, for the 4-year-olds, 5-year-olds, 7-year-olds, and adults, respectively. The latter three percentages, but not the first one, are significantly ($p < .001$) above chance expectations by t test. Pairwise t test comparisons between age groups on these percentages were all significant ($p < .05$), except for that between the 5- and the 7-year-olds. Chi-squares computed on the data for the two youngest groups combined versus the two oldest groups combined revealed significant ($p < .05$) age effects for the Listen, Read, Decide, and Future Negative situations. Expected cell frequencies were too low to do a chi-square test on the Past Negative data, but a Fisher's exact test showed a near-significant ($p < .06$) age difference for this situation also.

A similar 4 (age group) × 2 (situation: the leftmost five situations in Table 7 vs. the two emotionally negative situations) mixed analysis of variance was performed on subjects' plausible inferences in response to the follow-up question, "What might be going on in her mind?" This analysis yielded significant main effects for age ($F[3, 72] = 22.75, p < .001$) and for situation ($F[1, 72] = 21.89, p < .001$) plus a significant age × situation interaction ($F[3, 72] = 3.76, p < .01$). The percentages of plausible inferences across these seven tasks combined were 37%, 66%, 76%, and 97%, from youngest to oldest subject group. Again, all pairwise t test comparisons between groups were significant ($p < .01$), except between the two middle groups. Chi-square analyses showed significant ($p < .05$) increases with age for each of these seven situations. Contrary to what we thought might happen, subjects proved to be more rather than less likely to make a plausible inference in the two no-activity but negative situations (78%) than in the five activity ones (60%). However, this difference was found only in the

5-year-old group (84% vs. 48%) and the 7-year-old group (90% vs. 63%), hence the significant interaction effect.

As anticipated, subjects were more likely to say "yes" to the initial attribution question in the Past Negative than in the Neutral situation ($p < .01$, Sign test), and they were also more likely to do so in the Future Negative than in the Neutral situation ($p < .01$, Sign test). Also as expected, only a minority of subjects at each age attributed mental activity to a character said to be in a dreamless sleep; only in the 7-year-old group was this minority small enough to differ significantly from chance, however (see Table 7). Subjects' reluctance to attribute mental activity in this situation suggests that their willingness to do so in the others was not due to a simple tendency to say "yes" whenever the experimenter asked a yes-no mental attribution question.

The most important results of this study are the age differences. In the pretraining, subjects were given a broad and inclusive list of mental events as examples of "something going on in a person's mind": paying attention to, thinking that, thinking about, wondering, and feeling. Had they really thought that something mental—indeed, *anything* mental—was happening in the story characters' minds in the various situations, it is hard to see why they would not say so. Nevertheless, the 4-year-olds said that there was something going on in the story characters' minds on only 59% of the occasions when they should have. Even that 59% probably represents an overestimate of what they actually understood because on only 37% of the tasks did they both say that something was going on and also, when asked, make a reasonable situation-appropriate inference as to what it was: for example, say that the character listening to a story about elephants is thinking about the story, or about elephants, or about anything else that might plausibly be story related. Their 47% attribution level in the case of the Neutral situation (Table 7) is similar to that shown by 4-year-olds on the Wait trials in Flavell et al.'s (1993) three studies (43%, 38%, and 47%). This is further evidence that 4-year-olds are apt to believe that a person who is doing nothing overtly may also be doing nothing covertly.

More surprising was the 4-year-olds' low level of attribution (mean = 60%) and attribution plus plausible inference (mean = 32%) in the five situations in which the story character was very obviously doing something that requires some mental activity, that is, those situations in which the character was explicitly said to be listening, looking, reading, talking, and deciding. These results suggest that 4-year-olds may fail to infer the presence of mental activity, not only when the situation does not suggest any (Neutral, Wait situations), but also sometimes when it clearly does (the five situations mentioned above). We return to this possibility in Study 8, in which we attempted to make a better test of 4-year-olds' willingness or unwillingness to attribute mental activity to a person who is manifestly engaged in perceptual or intellectual activities.

The 5- and 7-year-olds were more likely than the 4-year-olds to respond affirmatively to attribution questions in all but the Asleep situation. They were also more likely to justify their affirmative answers with reasonable, situation-appropriate inferences as to the content of that mental activity (the figures in parentheses in Table 7). In the two situations entailing negative emotional experiences particularly, their performance rivaled that of the adults. They clearly understood that otherwise idle people may ruminate about past or future personal misfortunes. At the same time, they were often surprisingly poor at inferring the correct mental content in the Listen, Look, Read, and Talk situations. This raises the possibility, which we explore in Studies 9–14, that children are considerably less skilled than adults at inferring what a person is likely to be thinking from knowledge of what situation the person is in. That is, even when they are able to infer from situational cues *that* another person is thinking, they may be unable to infer from these cues *what* that thinking might be.

STUDY 8

It is not clear from our previous research just how likely young children are to attribute mental activity to a person known to be engaged in perceptual or intellectual activities. As regards perceptual activities, 90% of a 4-year-old group in Flavell et al.'s (1993) first study attributed mental activity to a person who was looking at pictures. In contrast, only 53% of the 4-year-olds in Study 7 did so (see the "Look" column of Table 7 above), a percentage not significantly greater than would be expected by chance. Likewise nonsignificant are the corresponding Study 7 percentages for a person who is listening (58%) and reading (53%). As to intellectual activities, in Flavell et al.'s (1993) first study, only 65% (nonsignificant) of the 4-year-olds attributed mental activity to a person engaged in problem solving. In Study 7, likewise, only 63% made this attribution to an individual who was trying to make a decision.

However, questions could be raised about both these sets of results. In Study 7, the individuals about whom the mental activity judgments were made were depicted rather than live; their static, pictorial appearance might have reduced the children's sense that mental activity was going on in these individuals. Although the target person was alive and physically present in Flavell et al.'s (1993) study, the Looking and Problem Solving trials in that study were always preceded by Wait trials, which may have affected the children's responses to the former trials in some way.

Consequently, one objective of the present study was to provide an additional, better test of 4-year-olds' disposition to attribute mentation to people engaged in perceptual and problem-solving activities. Accordingly, the target person was physically present rather than depicted, and the two types of situations were presented in counterbalanced rather than fixed order, to ensure that half the subjects would experience trials of each type with no other situations preceding them. Four-year-olds were given two Perceptual trials, in which an experimenter (E2) either viewed a picture book or listened to a tape recording, and two Problem Solving trials, in which she was asked either to make a decision or to prepare to explain how a large pear could fit through a small bottle opening. The test question was whether her mind was or was not doing anything in each of those situations.

The second objective was to make a different test of 4-year-olds' understanding of the stream of consciousness. The three Flavell et al. (1993) studies and Study 7 showed that 4-year-olds tend not to assume that a person who is just waiting quietly, not engaged in any task, must nevertheless still be experiencing some sort of mental content. We wondered what would happen if children of this age were presented with a waiting person and two opposing arguments on the matter and merely had to decide which argument was correct. One argument would be that something is always going on in people's minds and so there *must* be something going on in this inactive person's mind. The other would be that this person does not *look* as if anything were going on in her mind and so probably nothing is.

We reasoned that if 4-year-olds had even an intimation of the ever-flowing stream of consciousness they might be able to recognize and accept an explicit statement of it. Consequently, at the end of the testing sessions we asked subjects to choose between these two arguments on each of two Wait trials. In the first, E2 just waited quietly, facing away from the subject, as in the Flavell et al. (1993) studies. In the second, her eyes and ears were also covered while she waited. The latter was done both to introduce variety and to make E2 look even more overtly inactive. (Whether the covered eyes and ears actually made her seem any less *mentally* active is a matter of opinion. An observer could reason that they left her with nothing else to do *but* think.)

Method

Subjects

Subjects were 24 4-year-olds (mean age 4-7, range 4-1 to 4-11). The group consisted of 10 girls and 14 boys. All children were drawn from the same preschool population as the 4-year-olds in Study 7, but none had participated in that study. Two female experimenters tested the children.

Procedure

Pretraining.—As in Study 7, we began the session by acquainting the subjects with the wide range of brain or mind activities that could be included in the notion of an active mind. We wanted to ensure that the subjects understood that we did not just mean deliberate, directed problem-solving activity. One experimenter (E1) asked, "Do you know what your brain or mind does?" and paused for the child's reply. E1 continued, "I have a brain in my head [she pointed to her head], and you have a brain in your head. Brains or minds are important: they do a lot of things. We use them for figuring things out, for paying attention to what is happening around us, for deciding things, for remembering things, and even for knowing how we are feeling inside, like if we are feeling happy or sad. Sometimes our brains or minds seem to do things all by themselves. For example, new ideas or even memories just pop into our brains or minds without our even trying. Like, you'll be doing one thing and find yourself *thinking* about something else."

She then introduced two line drawings of heads. In one, the brain was outlined but was empty; in the other, it contained a short, uneven jagged line representing mental activity. E1 said, "Here's a picture of someone's head. This is where the brain or mind is. This picture shows a brain or mind that's *not doing* anything [E2 pointed to the empty space]. This other picture shows a brain or mind that *is doing* some things [she points to the line]—things like having ideas or feelings, or remembering." Children were then asked, "Which picture shows a mind that's *not doing* anything?" "Which picture shows a mind that *is doing* something?" Two children failed to answer these questions correctly, even after corrective feedback; they were dropped from the study. The remaining 24 subjects needed no corrective feedback.

Testing.—E1 was seated next to the child. The two Perceptual and two Problem Solving tasks were blocked and counterbalanced across subjects. Counterbalancing within blocks of tasks was achieved by the use of four basic task orders: 1, 2, 3, 4; 2, 1, 4, 3; 3, 4, 1, 2; and 4, 3, 2, 1. We systematically alternated the order of the choices within questions for each child from task to task and randomly placed the line drawings in left-right positions on the first block of tasks, switching their placement on the next block of tasks, and switching once again on the final two Wait tasks.

Perceptual tasks.—The procedure for the Perceptual tasks is illustrated by describing the picture book task. E2 asked E1 for permission to look at a picture book and then seated herself in a far corner of the testing room, facing a blank wall with her back to the child. From their viewing perspective, E1 and the subject could see only that E2 was turning the pages of the book. E1 then asked, "Ellie is over there looking at the picture book, isn't she? While she is looking at the picture book, is her mind like this [E1 pointed to a line drawing], *doing* something, or is her mind like this [E1 pointed to the other drawing], *not doing* anything? Which picture shows how her brain or mind is while she's looking at the picture book?"

On the other Perceptual trial E2 announced that she wanted to listen to a story on a tape, donned earphones, positioned herself in a different corner of the room, and announced that the tape was playing. The test question was as before, with the following alteration: "Ellie is over there listening to a story, isn't she? While she is listening to the story, is her mind . . . ?" E2 continued to sit in alternate corners of the room on subsequent trials.

Problem Solving tasks.—On the decision task, E2 faced E1 and the child, and E1 asked, "Ellie, would you please decide where we are going to eat lunch tomorrow. We could go to the fish restaurant or to the Chinese restaurant or to the hamburger place. Or we could eat at the student union or my house. Let me know when you have decided." E2 said, "Give me a minute," and seated herself, her back to the child. The test question was, "Ellie hasn't decided yet about where we are going to eat, has she? While she is deciding, is her mind like this, *not doing* anything, or is her mind like this, *doing* something? Which picture shows how her brain or mind is while she's deciding where to eat lunch?"

On the pear task, E1 presented a bottle of pear brandy and said, "Ellie, I have a mystery here. There is a very large pear in this bottle, but the opening at the top of this bottle is very tiny [E1 pointed to the bottle's skinny neck]. Can you tell us how the pear got in the bottle?" The remainder of the procedure was identical to that already described. The test question began with, "Ellie hasn't decided yet about how that pear got in the bottle, has she? While she is deciding . . . ?"

Wait tasks.—The final tasks were given in fixed order. E1 simply asked E2 to wait for a few moments without engaging in any specific activity. A varied form of the test question was introduced on these trials. On the standard Wait trial, E1 said, "Ellie, would you please go over to that chair and wait there for just a few minutes. We'll tell you when we are ready. Ellie is just waiting there, isn't she? I asked two different people about her mind when she was waiting there. One person said it doesn't *look like* anything is going on in her mind, so probably nothing is going on, like this [E1 pointed to the appropriate line drawing]. The other person said something is always going on in people's minds, so there *must* be something going on, like this [E1 pointed to the other drawing]. Which person is right? The one who said probably *nothing* is going on, or the one who said there *must* be something going on?" The next trial was very similar, except that E2 covered her ears and donned a blindfold, and E1 said, ". . . I asked two different people about her mind when she can't hear and can't see . . . ?" The ordering of the statements and question orders within test questions were alternated on each of these two trials.

Results and Discussion

Table 8 shows the percentages of subjects who said that E2's mind was "doing something" in the two Perceptual and Problem Solving situations and that there was "something going on" in her mind in the two Wait situations that followed. As the table shows, most of the subjects said that E2's mind was doing something in each of the two Problem Solving situations: 75% made this attribution in the situation when she was trying to decide where to eat (Decide), 89% when she was trying to solve the pear-in-the-bottle problem (Solve), and 75% in both situations; all three percentages are significantly greater than would be expected by chance. In contrast, none of the corresponding percentages are greater than chance expectation in the Perceptual situations: 46% for Look, 63% for Listen, and 33% for both. A 2 (tasks: Perceptual vs. Problem Solving) × 2 (order: Perceptual tasks first vs. Problem Solving tasks first) analysis of variance yielded as its only significant effect a main effect for task type ($F[1, 22] = 7.07, p < .01$). That is, children made significantly more mental attributions in Problem Solving than in Perceptual tasks, but there was no evidence that the order in which these two types of tasks were experienced significantly influenced how children responded to them.

The percentages of subjects in the two Wait situations siding with the view that something is always going on so there must be something going on were also not significantly above chance: 67% for the first (E2 just wait-

TABLE 8

PERCENTAGE OF 4-YEAR-OLDS ATTRIBUTING
MENTAL ACTIVITY TO E2 IN PERCEPTUAL,
PROBLEM SOLVING, AND WAIT
SITUATIONS IN STUDY 8

	Look	Listen
Perceptual	46	63
	Decide	Solve
Problem Solving	75*	88*
	Standard	Covered
Wait	67	58

NOTE.—Percentages significantly ($p < .05$) different from chance expectation of 50% by t test are marked with an asterisk.

ing), 58% for the second (E2 waiting with her eyes and ears covered), and 38% for both. Within-subject t tests showed that subjects' Wait attributions were not significantly different in frequency from their Perceptual ones but were significantly less frequent than their Problem Solving attributions ($t[23]$ = 2.39, p < .05). Of the 24 children, only four (17%) attributed mental activity in all four Perceptual and Wait situations, with three of these children also doing so in the Problem Solving situations and thus performing correctly on all six tasks. Finally, at the beginning of the pretraining, the children were asked, "Do you know what your brain or mind does?" Only seven subjects offered answers, but all seven were reasonable: five said, "Think"; one said, "It helps you talk"; and one said, "Sometimes it talks to me."

The data from the Problem Solving trials suggest that children of this age are disposed to think that a person's mind is active if there is clear evidence that the person is engaged in a prototypically mental activity such as decision making or problem solving. Consistent with this suggestion was the finding in Study 3 that almost all the 4-year-olds said "thinking" when asked what a reflective-looking E2 (who had just agreed to try to make a decision or solve a problem) was doing. At the same time, the lower attribution rates for similar situations obtained in the Flavell et al. (1993) study (65%) and in Study 7 (63%) suggest that this disposition is rather fragile and uncertain. We believe that their responses are probably dictated more by specific, here-and-now perceptual impressions than by any general, rule-like convictions about when the mind is active. That is, if what the children see and hear in a specific situation gives them the immediate sense that the other person is mentally active, they will affirm that the person is "having some thoughts and ideas," or that his or her mind is "doing something," or that "something is going on" in it—however the idea of mental activity happens to be conveyed in the particular study. In addition, it is very likely that some of their responses are just guesses, based on no particular impression.

The data from the Perceptual trials (and the Wait trials also) underscore this need to be cautious about how much understanding concerning the "when" of mental activity to grant children of this age. The Perceptual data, together with those of Study 7, suggest that they have no general, principled understanding that sustained perceptual-cognitive activities such as looking at pictures, listening to stories, and reading books require mental activity. In fact, the preponderance of evidence so far suggests that they are generally no more likely to attribute mentation to people engaged in these activities than to people who are not engaged in any task at all (the data for the one-trial Looking condition in the Flavell et al., 1993, study—90% attribution—being the only contrary evidence here).

The Problem Solving and Perceptual results of this study are also consistent with evidence obtained by Johnson and Wellman (1982) that children are more likely to think that you need your brain or mind to perform intellectual acts (e.g., think, remember) than to perform perceptual ones (e.g., see, hear) whereas adults recognize that they are necessary for both types of acts. A possibility, which we plan to test more systematically in future studies, is that young children believe that the eyes and ears are sufficient as well as necessary for seeing-looking and hearing-listening, respectively.

In our previous studies involving a Wait condition (Flavell et al., 1993, and Study 7), it is possible that 4-year-olds failed to attribute mental activity to the inactive person in part because, the person presenting no clues regarding mental activity, they could not imagine what its content might be. Not coming up with any hypotheses as to what she might be thinking, they may have just assumed that she probably was not having any thoughts or at least that it would be imprudent to assert that she was. In the present Wait trials, however, the attribution option was cast in a more abstract, general-rule-like form (". . . something is always going on in people's minds, so there *must* be something going on") that should have been less likely to set subjects to try to figure out what this particular person might be thinking at this particular moment.

With this possible problem eliminated in the present Wait trials, it is hard to see why a subject who really did sense that some sort of mental content is virtually always present in a conscious mind would not choose the option that presents this view on both these trials. In fact, however, three of the 24 subjects never chose it, 12 chose it on only one trial, and only nine chose it on both trials. One wonders even about the nine, in view of the fact that these subjects had attributed mental activity on only 61% of the Perception trials. These results suggest that the presence of this option did not cue any nascent intuitions about the stream of consciousness in most of the children. More likely, in most cases they either guessed, chose randomly, or were swayed by E2's inactive appearance into accepting the alternative, appearance-based argument.

We believe that these results constitute the most persuasive evidence to date that most young children do not have the notion of an essentially unceasing and unstoppable stream of consciousness as part of their naive theory of mind. As one 4-year-old said in response to some informal posttest questioning, "Every time you think for a little while, something goes on, and something goes off. Sometimes something goes on for a couple of minutes, and then a few minutes there is nothing going on." Another justified her choice of no mental activity on the second Wait trial by saying, "Because if she can't hear she doesn't get anything in her mind." However, one child in the group did say something that suggested some grasp of the notion of a stream of consciousness: "Because you think all the time."

STUDY 9

In Study 3 (Chap. II), 3- and 4-year-olds watched as E2 was presented with a problem, agreed to work on it ("Give me a minute," she said), and then looked deeply reflective, as if struggling to solve it. When asked what E2 was "doing," most of the 3-year-olds did not say "thinking," whereas most of the 4-year-olds did. Assuming that the 4-year-olds really did know from the strong cues provided *that* E2 was thinking, did they also know *what* she was thinking about?

One would assume that they must have known that she was thinking about the problem rather than about something else. However, there was no actual evidence that they did, and our subsequent studies have made us cautious about accepting untested assumptions regarding young children's knowledge about thinking. For example, the results of Study 7 (Table 7 above) provide some grounds for caution here: even when preschoolers attributed mental activity to a person engaged in mental endeavors like decision making or reading, they often failed to give plausible answers to the experimenter's follow-up content question, "What might be going on in her mind?" Similarly, Studies 11–14 (Chap. IV) show that they are often unable to use situational or other cues to reconstruct the content as well as the fact of their own thinking accurately. Finally, young children sometimes report that they (Studies 11–13, Chap. IV) or another person (Studies 4 and 6, Chap. II) had thought about objects that they or the other person clearly had not thought about, either instead of or in addition to reporting the person's true thought content.

The purpose of Studies 9 and 10 was to make further tests of preschoolers' ability to infer from rich situational and behavioral cues (*a*) that another person (E2) is currently thinking, (*b*) what she is thinking about, and (*c*) what she is not thinking about. There were two salient objects present in each task. E2 had attended to and commented on both of them just previously, evaluating one positively and the other negatively. There was also strong and clear evidence that she was currently wholly preoccupied with the negative object and not thinking about the positive one at all. We then assessed whether subjects knew what she was currently doing (answer: "thinking"), that she was thinking specifically about the negative object, and that she was not thinking about the positive object.

The children were then also tested for their recognition that E2 likes the positive object and does not like the negative object—the opposite of what she was and was not currently thinking about. We reasoned that, if they really did not know what she was and was not thinking about, they would find the positive object an attractive default option, either saying that the positive object was the only one she was thinking about (Study 9) or that—also incorrect—she was currently thinking about the positive object in addition to the negative one (Study 10). We expected the subjects to perform very well on the "likes" questions, if only because they could answer them correctly merely by reporting their own preferences. The question of interest was whether they would also do well on the structurally similar questions about the focus of her thinking.

The two tasks used in Study 9 were conceived of as being extremely easy tests of children's ability to infer the fact and content of another person's thought from very obvious situational and behavioral cues. We thought that even 3-year-olds might do fairly well on them and therefore included this age group in the subject sample.

Method

Subjects

Three groups of children served as subjects: 20 3-year-olds (10 of each sex, mean age 3-6, range 3-2 to 3-11), 20 4-year-olds (10 of each sex, mean age 4-6, range 4-0 to 4-11), and 20 5-year-olds (13 boys and seven girls, mean age 5-3, range 5-0 to 5-11). The children were drawn from several preschools and were mostly of upper-middle-class backgrounds.

Procedure

E1 sat next to the child across the table from E2. Because, as noted above, previous work had suggested that children sometimes claim that a person is thinking about more than one object or topic at a time, the experimenters demonstrated that E2 would be thinking only of one of two objects. As she placed two fairly interesting objects on the table, E1 said to E2, "Francie, I want to show you some things. Here is a bird, and here is a doll. I want you to close your eyes and think about just one of these things, and then we'll try to figure out which one you are thinking about."

E2 looked carefully at each item as it was presented, then covered her eyes with her hands and said, "OK. My eyes are closed, and I'm thinking about one of them. I'm remembering what color it is and how it looks. It has some blue on it [a property shared by both objects]. Which one am I thinking about?" E1 turned to the child and said, "Let's figure out which one she has in mind. What shall we say? Is she thinking about the bird or the doll?"

When the child had guessed one of the objects, E1 said to E2, "Are you thinking about the bird/doll?" E2 always indicated that the guess was incorrect: "No, I'm thinking about the doll/bird." By making the choice incorrect, we hoped to highlight further the fact that only one of the two objects was being thought about. E1 turned to the child and said, "Oh. She is thinking about the doll. She is *not* thinking about the bird. Which one is she thinking about? Good. Which one is she *not* thinking about? Good." If the child missed either question (very few did), the information was repeated. "Actually she is thinking about the doll, and she is *not* thinking about the bird." The questions were asked again, and the one 3-year-old who was again incorrect was dropped from the study. E1 removed the bird and doll from the table.

There were two tasks, Shirt and Water. The order of the two tasks was counterbalanced, the order of the questions within the tasks was fixed, and the relative positions of the objects placed on the table and the direction in which E2 turned when asked a question were randomly varied.

Shirt task.—E1 placed a very dirty, greasy T-shirt on the table and said to E2, "Francie, here are some more things to look at. Here is a *dirty* shirt." E2 responded, "That shirt is *yucky!* It is very dirty and full of grease! *Yuck!*" E1 then said, "Here is a *nice* flower," to which E2 responded, "That flower is *pretty!* It's a good color too." E2 looked at each object as she commented on it. E1 then said, "I have a question for you, Francie. How did that *yucky* stuff get all over that shirt?" E2 stared at the shirt, saying, "That's a hard question. Give me a minute. Hmmm." Looking thoughtful, she then turned 90° and rested her chin on her hand in a stereotypical "thinking" pose.

E1 asked all the children the general question, "What is Francie doing right now?" The questions that followed depended on the child's answer, as follows:

> If the child gave a complete answer to this general question, including the content of the thought, E1 repeated the child's response, "She's thinking about the shirt/the flower," and then asked, "Which one is she *not* thinking about?"
>
> If the child just answered "thinking" in response to the general question, E1 said, "She's thinking about just one of these two things [E1 pointed back and forth]. Which one is she thinking about? Which one is she *not* thinking about?"
>
> If the child gave any other answer or failed to answer the general question, E1 asked, "Is she thinking about anything right now or not?" If the child answered "yes," E1 said, "She's thinking about just one of these two things [E1 pointed back and forth]. Which one is she thinking about? Which one is she *not* thinking about?"

All children were then asked, "She likes just one of these two things [E1 pointed back and forth]. Which one does she like? Which one does she *not* like?"

Water task.—E1 introduced two more objects: "Francie, here are some more things to look at. Here is an *icky* glass of water." E2 responded, "That water is *awful!* I can't drink that! There's a fly and some dirt in there! *Ick!*" E1 placed a teddy bear on the table, saying, "Here is a *tiny* teddy bear." E2 said, "That teddy bear is *cute.* He's holding some tiny balloons too." E1 then asked E2 the problem question, "I have a question for you Francie. How did the *icky* stuff get in that glass of water?" E2's response and the test questions that followed were the same as those in the Shirt task.

Results and Discussion

Table 9 shows three sets of results: (*a*) the extent to which subjects of each age spontaneously said "thinking" when asked what pensive-looking E2 is doing on each task; (*b*) the extent to which they inferred correctly that she is thinking about the negative object rather than the positive one; and (*c*) the extent to which they inferred correctly that she likes the positive object rather than the negative one. There were no significant task-order effects for any of these measures.

As to *a,* the "Thinking" columns in the table show that even the youngest subjects were fairly good at inferring that E2 was thinking and that the two older groups were somewhat (nonsignificantly) better. Of the 20 subjects in each group, 12 3-year-olds, 16 4-year-olds, and 16 5-year-olds gave the "thinking" answer in response to E1's initial question ("What is Francie doing right now?") on both tasks. In addition, in response to the follow-up question, "Is she thinking about anything right now or not?" only eight 3-year-olds, no 4-year-olds, and three 5-year-olds ever said that E2 was not thinking or that they did not know whether she was. Granted that the idea of thinking and the word *thinking* were primed during the pretest, this still

TABLE 9

PERCENTAGE "THINKING" RESPONSE TO THE QUESTION, "WHAT IS E2 DOING?" AND
CORRECT IDENTIFICATION OF WHAT SHE IS THINKING ABOUT AND LIKES IN STUDY 9

	TASK					
	Shirt			Water		
AGE	"Thinking"	Think	Like	"Thinking"	Think	Like
3	75	70	90	60	50	85
4	90	60	95	85	50	75
5	80	60	100	90	75	100

seems a rather impressive performance. Consistent with Studies 3 and 8 and the studies cited in Study 3 (Baron-Cohen & Cross, 1992; Rosenkrantz, 1991), these findings suggest that preschoolers are capable of inferring that a person is thinking about something from very strong situational and— especially, we suspect—behavioral cues (e.g., the stereotypical thinking pose).

As to b, the "Think" columns in Table 9 show the percentages of children at each age and on each task who correctly answered the critical question, "Which one is she thinking about?" (They virtually always selected the other, remaining object in response to the subsequent question, "Which one is she *not* thinking about?" Consequently, children's responses to the latter question were therefore redundant and are not considered further.) These data suggest that subjects of all three ages tended to be quite poor at inferring what object E2 was thinking about from the very strong evidence provided, namely, from the explicit statement of the problem concerning that object and E2's obvious (to adults, at least) agreement to ponder it. The percentages in these columns range from 50% to 75%, with a mean of 61%, results not significantly higher than would be expected by chance. The percentages of subjects correctly choosing the negative object on both trials were 50%, 45%, and 55%, from youngest to oldest group. On 107 of the 120 total trials, subjects agreed, initially or subsequently, that E2 was thinking. But, on 34 (or 32%) of these 107, subjects went on to misidentify the object of her thinking—a substantial number considering how easy it should have been for them to make the right choice.

Of course this does not mean that none of the subjects knew what E2 was thinking about. On the contrary, on at least one trial, in response to E2's initial question, "What is Francie doing right now?" 16 subjects (six 3-year-olds, four 4-year-olds, and six 5-year-olds) correctly said that E2 was thinking about the negative object immediately; moreover, seven of these did so on both trials. On the other hand, the majority of the subjects at all three age levels displayed what seemed at most to be a limited ability to infer the focus of her thought from the rich evidence available.

Finally, in contrast to the "Think"-column results, the "Like" columns of Table 9 show that most subjects had little difficulty inferring which objects E2 liked and disliked (or, quite possibly, simply which objects seemed objectively desirable to them and which ones did not). A 3 (age) × 2 (task type) mixed analysis of variance yielded as its only significant result a main effect for task type ($F[1, 57] = 19.08$, $p < .001$). This analysis shows that there was no significant improvement with age on the think and like tasks but that subjects of all ages performed significantly better on the latter than on the former. In summary, the results of this study suggest that, given abundant evidence, 3–5-year-old children can be quite good at inferring *that* another person is thinking but surprisingly poor at inferring *what* that person is thinking about.

STUDY 10

One reason for children's poor performance in the previous study might have been that, although we did provide sufficiently strong behavioral evidence *that* E2 was thinking, we failed to provide sufficiently strong cues to permit them to infer the *content* of her thought. Subjects were forced to draw an inference as to the content of her thought and often drew on their knowledge of her personal preference for one of the objects rather than their knowledge that she had just been asked a specific question about one of the objects. Accordingly, in the new study we sought to provide even stronger cues as to what E2 was and was not thinking about by having her touch and visually inspect the target object, and only that object, at the time of the test questions. Given such unequivocal evidence for the object of E2's thought, we expected that subjects would (*a*) not assume that she was thinking primarily of the nontarget, salient, but physically attractive object and (*b*) also not agree that she was thinking of both objects simultaneously. We felt that success on the new tasks would suggest some understanding of thinking and mental attention (although, given the confound of thinking with touching and visual inspection, we would not know exactly how much). On the other hand, failure on these extremely easy tasks would suggest very limited understanding indeed.

Several alterations in the procedures of the previous study were made to test these expectations. In the pretest period we attempted to get subjects to generate examples of their thinking and introduced some other needed changes. The two tasks were very similar to the two tasks of the previous study, with the following exceptions: (*a*) As previously noted, we gave extreme behavioral evidence as to the content of E2's thought. (*b*) We asked a different test question, of the form, "Is she just thinking about the *x*, or is she thinking about the *y* too?" (*c*) We asked the "like" questions only on a subject's second task. (*d*) We also asked only on that second task whether E2 was also thinking about a physically present but previously unmentioned and nonsalient object.

Two other tasks were given at the end of the session, the first to probe subjects' understanding of mental-attentional limitations, the second as a further test of their introspective abilities—*further* because, although this study belongs in this chapter, it was actually carried out after the introspection studies reported in the next chapter. In the former, two line drawings of thought bubbles were used to ask whether the children believed that a person would have only one thought or many thoughts during a brief moment of time. In the latter, subjects were asked while working puzzles whether they were currently thinking about anything.

Method

Subjects

Subjects were 20 4-year-olds (mean age 4-4, range 4-0 to 4-10) and 20 5-year-olds (mean age 5-3, range 5-0 to 5-7). There were eight girls and 12 boys in the younger group and an equal number of girls and boys in the older group. The children were drawn from one of the preschools used in the previous study and were of mostly upper-middle-class backgrounds. None had participated in the previous study. All were tested by the same experimenters as before, taking the same experimental roles.

Procedure

Pretest.—E1 sat next to the child, with E2 sitting across the testing table. The child was first given practice answering questions of the same form as the test question. A book and a battery were placed on the table, and E2 picked up just the battery. E1 said, "Francie is holding the battery, isn't she? Is she holding the book too, or is she just holding the battery?" Next, E2 was presented with a crayon and a pencil, and she picked up both. E1 asked, "Francie is holding the crayon, isn't she? Is she just holding the crayon, or is she holding the pencil too?" Only one child had some trouble with the question format. After corrective feedback, E1 repeated the questions, and he answered correctly. No child was excluded from the study.

E1 then introduced the notion of thinking to the child in the following manner: "In the game today we are going to talk about thinking. I think about things a lot of the time, especially when I'm sitting quietly by myself or trying to go to sleep at night. I think about this, and I think about that. I have thoughts about this and thoughts about that." The child was then asked, "How about you? When you are sitting quietly or trying to go to sleep, do you think about things?" If the answer was "yes," E1 asked, "What kinds of things do you think about?" Regardless of the child's previous replies, E1 then asked, "Are there other times of the day when you think about things? When's that? What kinds of things do you think about?"

Test.—The Shirt and Water tasks were retained from the previous study and counterbalanced as before. The two stimuli for each task were presented to E2 in the same fashion, and E2 commented on them both in the same manner. Changes in the procedure are illustrated for the Shirt task.

After being asked by E1, "How did that *yucky* stuff get all over the shirt?" E2 said, as before, "That's a hard question. Give me a minute. Hmmm." Rather than turning away as in Study 9, however, E2 put her hand on her chin in a reflective pose, stared at the shirt, and pursed her mouth. She also touched the shirt periodically as if to inspect it and kept doing all these things as the test questions were asked. Children were first asked, "What is Francie doing right now?" The following questions were then asked if they had not been answered by the response to an earlier question: "Is she thinking right now or not?" "What is she thinking about?" All children who agreed that she was thinking were finally asked, "Is she just thinking about the shirt/flower, or is she thinking about the flower/shirt too?" or, "Is she thinking about the flower/shirt too, or is she just thinking about the shirt/flower?"

Posttest questions.—While E2 was still inspecting the target on the subject's second task, E1 repeated the child's final answer to the forced choice thinking question and then asked if the subject was also thinking about her eyeglasses, a physically present but nonsalient object. For example, "You said she is thinking about the shirt/flower right now. Is she just thinking about the shirt/flower, or is she thinking about my eyeglasses too?" Next, the child was asked preference questions about the two basic stimuli in the task, the shirt and the flower: "Which one [E1 points] does she like? Does she like the shirt/flower too, or does she just like the flower/shirt?"

Two line drawings were constructed with thought bubbles appearing above a character's head. One thought bubble contained six asterisks to represent thoughts, and the other contained only one. The child was asked, "If somebody is thinking for just a teeny short bit of time, for just a second, does their head look like this [one drawing was placed in front of the child] with just one thought, or does it look like this [the other drawing was placed in front of the child] with lots of different thoughts happening all at the same time?" All orders of choices within posttest questions were counterbalanced.

Finally, each child was allowed to select a puzzle to work for fun. The task was to place small pieces on top of their pictorial matches in a large scene, such as a jungle. While the subject was attempting to match a piece, E2 asked, "Right now, are you thinking about anything or not?" If the answer was "yes," she asked, "What are you thinking about?" If it was "no," after an interval of time, she asked, "Right now, are you thinking about that puzzle or not?"

Results and Discussion

During the pretest, the children were asked if they think about things when sitting quietly or trying to go to sleep. Only 11 of the 20 4-year-olds said that they did, and of these 11 only seven could recall any specific examples. The corresponding figures for the 5-year-olds were 17 and eight. A few of their examples of thoughts both rang true and suggested some understanding of the meaning of *thinking about:* for example, "Well, I think about scary things, and then I don't go to sleep," and, "What I'm going to do when I get older."

Table 10 shows the percentages of 4- and 5-year-olds responding correctly to various test and posttest questions. As in Study 9, most of the 5-year-olds correctly responded "thinking" to E1's initial question, "What is Francie doing right now?" and the few who did not (two per task) said "yes" in response to the ensuing question, "Is she thinking right now or not?" In contrast to these results and those of Study 9, however, an average of only 55% of the 4-year-olds initially said "thinking," and three subjects also did not say "yes" in response to that ensuing question on one or both tasks. The difference between the two groups on the "thinking" measure is significant ($F[1, 38] = 10.95, p < .01$).

This performance may not reflect quite so negatively on the 4-year-olds' knowledge as it sounds, however. On eight trials, 4-year-olds said that E2 was "looking" instead of saying that she was "thinking"; on another trial, one 4-year-old said that she was "touching it." Likewise, on the four trials on which 5-year-olds did not say "thinking," they also said "looking" instead. Although probably reflecting less sensitivity to E2's current mental state than a "thinking" response would, these other responses are nonetheless correct answers to the "doing" question because, unlike the case in Study 9, in this study E2 was in fact staring at and occasionally touching the target object. Furthermore, whereas only 35% of the 4-year-olds responded "thinking" on whichever of the two tasks they experienced first, 75% did so on their second task. All the talk about thinking on their first task may have led some of them to focus more on E2's thinking than on her looking or touching on their second task (although we have not seen such effects of previous experience in previous studies).

Table 10 also shows that the 5-year-olds also answered most of the other questions correctly. Almost all of them correctly said that E2 was thinking about the negative, problematic object that she was inspecting (a glass of water or a shirt) and was not also thinking about E1's glasses. On the other hand, the first two "Other Too?" columns show that 5-year-olds did not always understand that she was not also thinking about an unattended-to object more salient than the glasses, namely, the positive object that she had previously noticed and commented on (a flower, a teddy bear). Despite what an adult would regard as indisputable evidence for total cognitive absorption with the negative object (tacitly agreeing to ponder it, continually staring at it and only it, and occasionally touching it), on 25%–30% of the tasks the 5-year-olds said that she was also or instead thinking about

TABLE 10

PERCENTAGE CORRECT RESPONSES TO SHIRT, WATER, AND POSTTEST QUESTIONS IN STUDY 10

AGE	SHIRT			WATER			POSTTEST		
	"Thinking"	Think	Other Too?	"Thinking"	Think	Other Too?	Glasses	Like	Other Too?
4	45	75	55	65	70	55	85	95	95
5	90	95	70	90	95	75	95	95	90

the positive one. This many errors, together with the not insubstantial number of "think" errors recorded in the preceding study (Table 9 above), suggests that 5-year-olds are still developing their ability to infer the focus of a person's mental attention from behavioral and situational cues and also, possibly, their very conception of selective, focused mental attention.

This conclusion is even more justified in the case of 4-year-olds. Although they did not perform significantly more poorly than the 5-year-olds on all measures, as a group they showed a decidedly limited ability to infer E2's mental-attentional focus and nonfocus from very obvious clues. Only nine of the 20 4-year-olds (vs. 13 5-year-olds, N.S.) correctly answered all four "think" and "other too?" questions; the comparable figures for three out of four correct answers were nine and 16 ($\chi^2[1]$ = 5.23, $p < .05$). Like the 5-year-olds, however, they seemed little tempted to say that E2 was also thinking about E1's eyeglasses. Furthermore, both groups had little difficulty inferring that E2 liked the positive object but did not also like the negative one. As in Study 9, the direction of E2's desires was easier for subjects to ascertain than the direction of her thoughts.

We thought that one reason that subjects might be inclined to say that E2 was thinking about the positive object as well as the negative one was that they are relatively unaware of limitations on people's attentional capacity. Recall that a similar argument was presented in Study 4 (Chap. II) to account for children's tendency to say that E2 was thinking of both the target and the distractor rather than just the target. The purpose of the "thought bubbles" test near the end of the testing session was thus to obtain some preliminary developmental data on children's understanding of attentional limitations. The results were that only 12 (60%) of the 4-year-olds but 18 (90%) of the 5-year-olds said that a person who was thinking would have only one thought rather than many in his or her head during a very brief period of time ($\chi^2[1]$ = 4.80, $p < .05$). The 4-year-olds' pattern of choices is not significantly different from chance, whereas that of the 5-year-olds is ($p < .01$, by Sign test).

The 5-year-olds, but not the 4-year-olds, were also asked why they chose the particular thought bubble they did. While most of their answers did not go beyond describing their choice, a few seemed to express some genuine intuitions about attentional limitations. Two examples were, "You can only think of one thing at a time," and, "Because you can't think of everything at the same time—you'll get confused." These data are consistent with Pillow's (1988, 1989a) evidence of improvement over the preschool and early elementary school period in children's understanding of attentional selectivity and attentional limits. However, the correlation within the 4-year-old group between performances on the Shirt and the Water tasks and the selection of the one-thought thought bubble proved to be only a nonsignificant .24 (ceiling effects made it inappropriate to compute this correlation for the

5-year-old group). We are planning to investigate young children's understanding of attentional focus and attentional limits in greater depth in future research.

In the final task, while the children were attempting to match their puzzle pieces, they were asked whether they were thinking about anything right then. This task was similar to those used in Study 14 (Chap. IV), in that it tested for on-line introspections of present thoughts rather than retrospections of recent ones. There were some interesting differences between the two age groups' responses to this task. Of the 20 4-year-olds, only 10 (50%) said that they were thinking. Moreover, when asked what they were thinking about, only five of those 10 referred to something currently problematic that they would in fact likely be thinking of at that moment, for example, "Thinking about where it [a particular piece] goes." Of the others, four referred to a puzzle piece that had already been put in place, and therefore needed no further thought, and one said that she did not know.

In the 5-year-old group, on the other hand, 14 subjects (70%) said that they were thinking, and all 14 went on to give plausible descriptions of what they were currently thinking, for example, "Thinking where is the animal I am looking for," and, "Trying to think where the footprints are." This group difference in frequency of plausible introspections (4 vs. 14) is significant ($\chi^2[1] = 8.12$, $p < .01$). Thus, 5-year-olds performed somewhat better on this introspection task than on those of Study 14 and definitely better than on those of Studies 11, 12, and 13. Asking subjects whether they were thinking about anything right at the moment that they were actively searching for a match in an engaging puzzle task, especially following an entire session devoted to talk about thinking, may have made it easier for them to report their thoughts than seems normally to be the case with 5-year-olds, at least as based on our other introspection studies. We now consider these other introspection studies.

IV. INTROSPECTION STUDIES

Our research strongly suggests that young children underattribute mental activity in a variety of situations (Chap. III; Flavell et al., 1993). They are less likely than older subjects to attribute mental activity to people who are just waiting, not engaged in any task. They are also less likely to attribute it to people who are obviously engaged in perceptual and sometimes even in intellectual tasks. Why such underestimates? One possibility raised by Flavell et al. (1993) is that young children lack the disposition and the ability to introspect. Lacking introspective skills, they would be unlikely spontaneously to notice and reflect on their own mental experiences and, consequently, unlikely to attribute such experiences to others, except perhaps when the situational or behavioral evidence for them is very clear.

Although it is a common assumption that young children are relatively lacking in introspective skills, we have found surprisingly little research evidence on the matter. Piaget's (1976) investigations of the development of consciousness are well known, but they actually dealt mostly with subjects' reflective awareness of their physical actions rather than their mental events. More germane is recent research by Gopnik and her colleagues (Gopnik & Astington, 1988; Gopnik & Slaughter, 1991).

Gopnik and Slaughter (1991) first induced various mental states (beliefs, pretenses, images, perceptions, desires, and intentions) in 3- and 4-year-olds and had the children verbally identify these states; they then caused the states to change and finally asked the children what their original states had been. In the case of beliefs, for example, the experimenters first showed the children a familiar crayon box and asked them what they thought was in it (all subjects said "crayons"); they then showed them that it actually contained candles rather than crayons and asked them what they had initially thought was in the box when they first saw it—crayons or candles. The 4-year-olds were quite accurate at reporting all their initial, previously verbalized mental states, including their initial false beliefs. The 3-year-olds recalled their initial pretenses, images, and perceptions very well, their initial desires and intentions less well, and—consistent with previous developmental research on false beliefs—their initial beliefs quite poorly. Baron-Cohen (1991) conducted a similar study with 4-year-olds and obtained similar results.

As Gopnik and Astington (1988) themselves noted, however, subjects could have succeeded on these tasks by simply recalling what they had said previously, rather than by actually recalling their previous mental states. On this point, earlier studies (Gopnik & Astington, 1988) had made similar tests for belief changes, but without asking subjects to verbalize their initial (false) beliefs at the outset. Although there was significant improvement from 3 to 5 years of age in subjects' ability to report accurately their initial but previously nonverbalized beliefs, the 4-year-olds were correct on only about 55%–60% of the trials and the 5-year-olds on only 70%–75%. It seems possible, therefore, that at least some of the children in the Baron-Cohen (1991) and Gopnik and Slaughter (1991) studies may have simply recalled their initial overt statements rather than having actually recalled or reconstructed their initial covert mental states. Similarly, it is also possible that, even when young children correctly reported what they saw, wanted, believed, etc. in the Gopnik and the Baron-Cohen studies, they may not have been aware that they were reporting mental events as opposed to the physical events to which the mental events often referred (see the concluding section of this chapter).

In this connection, likewise, research by Johnson and her colleagues (e.g., Foley & Johnson, 1985; Johnson, Hashtroudi, & Lindsay, 1993; Lindsay, Johnson, & Kwon, 1991) has shown that young children are less able than older children and adults to distinguish in memory what they had previously actually said or done from what they had previously only imagined saying or doing. For example, they might have trouble recalling whether they had really touched their nose in the recent past or had just imagined touching it. It is possible that young children may not spontaneously encode an action as being mental rather than nonmental in as distinctive and memorable a fashion as do older people. If so, they might be expected to be poorer at remembering what they had recently been thinking.

The only other directly relevant study by other investigators that we have found is a recent one by Estes and Buchanan (1993). They gave 4-, 5-, 6-, and 20-year-old subjects 56 trials of experience with a computer game in which Shepard-type mental rotation was a useful solution strategy. On each trial, subjects were to judge as quickly as possible whether two monkeys presented in different spatial orientations on the computer screen were holding up the same arm or different arms. No mention was made of the mental rotation strategy by the experimenter. Following the fifth, middle, and final trials, the experimenter questioned the subjects briefly about how they had made their judgments.

The investigators observed an increase with age in the percentage of subjects whose reaction time patterns indicated that they had mentally rotated one monkey in order to compare it with the other one. More to the present point, they also found a marked increase with age in the percentage of these "rotaters" who, when questioned, showed some awareness that they had been using a mental rotation strategy. The biggest increases in both measures occurred between 4 and 6 years, with the 6-year-olds being quite similar to the adults on both strategy use and awareness of strategy use. In addition, some of the 4- and 5-year-old rotaters who did not indicate any awareness of the rotation strategy specifically did make reference to some general mental activity such as thinking or imagining, for example, "I have to think real hard, but then I can tell." The percentages of rotaters specifically citing the rotation strategy were 14 (one subject), 57, 85, and 80 from youngest to oldest age group. This study suggests that some 5-year-olds, and more 6-year-olds, are capable of noticing some of their own mental actions, especially perhaps when the same action occurs again and again over the course of a long series of trials.

Finally, in the third of Flavell et al.'s (1993) studies, 16 4-year-old subjects were given a turn at waiting quietly for 8–10 sec while sitting in a corner facing a blank wall, just as they had seen the experimenter do previously. When questioned almost immediately afterward as to whether their minds had been "doing anything" during this waiting period, seven of the 16 said that they had not. Moreover, most of the thoughts reported by those who said that they had seemed more likely to have been present inventions stimulated by the experimenter's query than genuine memories of previous mental events. Thus, the subjects in that study proved to be no better at reporting that their own minds had been active than they were at inferring activity in the mind of another person in a similar waiting situation.

The purpose of the four studies reported in this chapter was to explore in greater depth young children's introspective abilities. Given the relatively poor performance of 4-year-olds in the Flavell et al. (1993) study just described, we decided to begin by testing 5-year-olds; 7–8-year-olds were also tested in Studies 12 and 13 for comparison purposes.

Three strategies guided the choice of tasks in the four studies. The first was always to ask the children to introspect about very recent periods of time in which we could know both *that* they had been thinking actively and at least roughly *what* the content of that thinking must have been. This was accomplished by first presenting them with interesting objects and events designed to stimulate a limited class of thoughts (without, however, explicitly telling the children to "think about" anything), then asking them to say whether they had been thinking about anything during this stimulus presentation period and, if so, what they had been thinking about. The use of this strategy ensured that the children would have something definite to introspect about, unlike the case in the Flavell et al. (1993) study mentioned above, and also allowed us to assess at least roughly the validity of the children's introspective reports.

The second strategy was to make the introspection tasks as easy as possible for young subjects. We tried to do this in various ways—by careful explanation and pretraining concerning what it meant to think about something, by causing the children to have thoughts that should be salient and easy to recall or reconstruct, by testing recall of these thoughts soon after the children had had them, and by modeling correct answers. The third strategy was to use a variety of different tasks over the four studies to increase our chances of detecting any beginning introspective competencies that children of this age might possess.

Thus, the second and third strategies were designed to increase the likelihood that accurate introspection would occur, and the first was designed to help us identify it when it did occur. In all four studies, we attempted to find out both whether the children know *that they had been* thinking and, if they said that they had been, whether they knew *what* they had been thinking about.

STUDY 11

Method

Subjects

Sixteen 5-year-olds, 10 boys and six girls, were tested. The mean age for the children was 5-5 (range 5-0 to 5-11). These children were drawn from a university laboratory preschool and were mostly from upper-middle-class backgrounds. Most of the subjects used in Studies 11–14 were white and native born, but exact demographic information on them was not available. All testing in these studies was conducted by the same female experimenter (E1), assisted by a second female experimenter (E2). No child participated in more than one of the four studies.

Procedure

A brief warm-up period was included to convey the meaning of *thinking about* something. The first experimenter (E1) began by placing a toy bear and a toy lion on the table. Then, looking at the ceiling, she told the child that she was thinking about one of them. The child was asked, "Which animal am I thinking about?" She continued, "That's right. I was thinking about [whichever one the child chose]. Now I am going to think about the other one. [She looked toward the ceiling.] Which animal am I thinking about? That's right. Good."

There were three tasks, two essentially identical ones that were always given first (Crayon, Soap), followed by a third, slightly different one (Bathroom). In each task, the children first sat in one place and were presented with a problem or a question that required them to think about certain target objects. Then they moved to a different seat and were asked whether they had been thinking about anything while they were sitting in the first location. After this open-ended question they were asked more specifically whether they had been thinking about the target objects if they had not already mentioned them (the correct answer was "yes") and also whether they had been thinking about two other "decoy" objects that they would not have been thinking about (the correct answer was "no"). The children also held an object in their hand while seated in the first place and were subsequently tested for recall of that action; this allowed us to compare in a rough way their memory for prior physical and mental events.

The two initial tasks were given in counterbalanced order, with corrective feedback provided after whichever one the child received first. The tasks are illustrated by describing the Crayon task.

First E1 asked the child and the second experimenter (E2) each to hold an envelope; she then placed a closed paper bag on the table. The child was then told, "I have two crayons to show you. One is longer, and one is shorter." E1 then held the crayons up at a distance from one another sufficient for E2 to note gross eye movements by the subject from one object to the other. E1 waited about 2 sec and asked, "Which one is the longer one?" The child chose, and E1 drew attention to each object, saying, "OK, you decided this is the longer one and this is the shorter one." Holding them side by side, she continued, "Actually/You are right, this is the longer one, and this is the shorter one." (The crayons were nearly the same length—8 cm and 8.36 cm—and subjects often guessed incorrectly.)

The subject and E2 were asked to place their envelopes down and to move to chairs located at the opposite end of the long table. The crayons and envelopes were placed before the subject, and E1 opened the paper bag, commenting, "Let's find out what is in this paper bag. Oh. A little doll." The doll was placed on the table with the other stimuli. The basic test question to the child was, "While you were sitting over there in that other chair [E1 pointed to the previous location], were you thinking about anything?" If the child said "yes," she said, "What were you thinking about while you were sitting in that chair?" and then, "Is there anything else you were thinking about?" The child was then queried only about items not mentioned spontaneously following these open-ended questions.

Each subject was questioned in an individually determined random order that was identical for each of the first two tasks. The basic query was, "While you were sitting over there, were you thinking about this x [pointing to one of the stimuli]?" The stimuli were the longer crayon and the shorter crayon (the two target objects) plus the previously hidden doll and an irrelevant object, E1's eyeglasses (the two decoy objects). The subject was also asked, "While you were sitting over there, were you holding anything in your hand?" If the response was "yes," the next question was, "What were you holding in your hand?" If the response was "no," the next question was, "Were you holding an envelope in your hand?"

Following the child's first task, E2 provided corrective feedback by modeling correct responses to the same questions. We thought that this corrective feedback might improve performance on the child's second task. The feedback is illustrated for the Crayons task. E2 was asked if she had been thinking about the longer crayon, and she replied, "Yes, I was. And while I was deciding that that one was the longer crayon I was also thinking about the shorter crayon too." Her answer to the question about the hidden object was, "No, I wasn't thinking about this doll. I didn't know about that doll when I was sitting over there." Her response to the irrelevant (eyeglasses) question was, "No, I wasn't thinking about them. I don't remember noticing them." Finally, she correctly stated that she had been holding an envelope in her hand.

For the similar Soap task, the comparison stimuli were two bars of soap, one real and the other fake. The hidden decoy object was a small ball containing water, and the irrelevant decoy object was E1's name tag. The child and E2 were asked to hold plastic cups while the child decided which soap was the real one.

Except for the manner in which we attempted to gain experimental control over the child's prior thoughts, the final, Bathroom task was identical in format to the previous two. The hidden object was a picture of a giraffe, the irrelevant object E1's shirt, and the object held an unsharpened pencil. E1 asked the child to sit on the carpet and hold the pencil. Then she said, "I'm going to ask you a question, but I don't want you to say the answer out loud. Keep the answer a secret, OK? Most people in the world have toothbrushes in their houses. They put their toothbrushes in a special room. Now don't say anything out loud. Keep it a secret. Which room in your house has your toothbrush in it?" She placed her finger to her lips and said, "Sssh." The child was then asked to return to the testing table, and the picture of the giraffe was unveiled. Following the child's response to the open-ended question, additional questions were asked about thinking about the decoy objects (giraffe, shirt) and the target object (bathroom). The purpose of this task was to see whether children would report having thought about an object that was never physically present—neither when first thought about nor during the subsequent recall probes.

Results and Discussion

Children's responses to the initial, open-ended thinking questions were assigned to one of three categories:

> *a) Target.*—Reported thoughts about both crayons, about both the real and the fake soaps, and about either a bathroom or a toothbrush (recall of either one was judged sufficient);
> *b) Other.*—Reported thoughts about anything else;
> *c) None.*—Denied any thoughts.

Table 11 shows the percentages of subjects scored for each of these categories (mental events) and also the percentages correctly recalling what object they had held in their hand (physical events).

It is apparent that the children were poor at recalling what should have been quite memorable or easily reconstructible mental events that had occurred only a minute or two previously. The numbers of children correctly reporting target thoughts on three, two, one, and none of the three tasks were none, three, four, and nine, respectively; moreover, on each task, 44%–63% of the children denied having had any thoughts of any kind. Although children's recall of the physical events was also not very impressive, it was distinctly superior to that of the mental events. Of the 16 subjects, 11 correctly recalled a higher percentage of physical events than (target) mental ones, no subject showed the reverse pattern, and five recalled the two types of events equally well ($p < .01$, by Sign test). This suggests that, although general memory limitations could have partly accounted for subjects' difficulties in recalling the mental events, they could not be the whole explanation.

Table 12 shows the percentages of subjects correctly recognizing that they had thought about the targets, had not thought about the decoys (hidden and irrelevant), and had held the specified objects. The children were quite good at recognizing that they had not thought about the decoy objects, suggesting that they were not indiscriminately agreeing with all suggestions

TABLE 11

PERCENTAGE RECALL OF MENTAL AND PHYSICAL
EVENTS IN STUDY 11

| TASK | MENTAL EVENTS | | | PHYSICAL EVENTS |
	Target	Other	None	
Crayon	19	38	44	50
Soap	13	44	44	63
Bathroom	31	6	63	88

TABLE 12

PERCENTAGE CORRECT RECOGNITION/REJECTION OF MENTAL AND PHYSICAL
EVENTS IN STUDY 11

TASK	MENTAL EVENTS					PHYSICAL EVENTS
	Target 1	Target 2	Hidden	Irrelevant	All	
Crayon	69	56	94	88	19	100
Soap	81	63	63	88	38	100
Bathroom	63	...	94	100	63	100

as to what they might have thought about. Quite the contrary, the first two columns of the table show that they said "yes" to an average of only 66% of the recognition questions concerning the target items. While definitely better than their free recall of target-object thoughts (Table 11 above), this still could not be regarded as very good recognition memory for previous thoughts.

Their performance level appears lower yet if one counts only correct recognition of both targets coupled with correct rejection of both decoys, as shown in the "All" column of Table 12. Consistent with the recall results, mean recognition of previous physical events (100%) was significantly better than mean recognition of previous mental events (66%) ($t[15] = 4.99, p < .001$).

Finally, there was no suggestion in the data that E2's modeling of the correct answers to recognition questions on the subjects' first task had any beneficial effect on their recall or recognition performance on their second task. That is, hearing her explain that she had thought about both the chosen and the nonchosen targets, but had not thought about either decoy, did not increase the likelihood that the subject would do the same on a similar task given immediately afterward. This modeling of correct answers should have made it clear to the children that they had "thought about" something if they had attended to it while sitting in the other chair. E2 was able to observe that all the children had in fact looked at both the longer (target 1) and the shorter (target 2) crayon in the Crayon task, and at both the real (target 1) and the fake (target 2) soap in the Soap test, before making their decision as to which was longer or which was real. Nevertheless, the most common error pattern in the recognition data was for children to say that they had previously thought about only one of the two targets, usually either the actually longer/real object (i.e., target 1) or the one the child had initially judged to be longer/real. This suggests that some of the children might have been equating thinking with mental products (the final answer) rather than with mental processes (the mental steps leading up to the final answer). We discuss this possibility again in Chapter V. Another possible explanation for this error pattern is that it may simply have been harder for them to recall or reconstruct that they had also attended to the nonchosen or incorrect target. Whatever their merits with respect to the Crayon and Soap tasks, such explanations could not account for subjects' almost equally poor performance on the Bathroom task. The reason is that only one object (either toothbrush or bathroom) needed to be reported on that task to be scored as correct (target) recall.

STUDY 12

We thought it possible that the poor performance by subjects on Study 11 might have resulted in part from our somewhat cursory pretraining in that study as to what was meant by *thinking about* an object. Had they had better pretraining on the notion that *thinking about* means "brief mental attention to," they might have been able to profit from E2's modeling of correct performance. In Study 12, we tried to improve the pretraining by conveying what was meant by *brief mental attention to an object* without relying solely on the expression *thinking about.* To accomplish this, we used a metaphor for the mind of a flashlight shining on an object and equated it with *thinking about* the object. A second purpose of this study was to compare the performance of 5-year-olds with that of older, early elementary school children. Other than the addition of the extended pretraining session and a slightly altered open-ended test question, the materials and procedures were identical to those of Study 11.

Method

Subjects

Two groups of children were tested, with 16 subjects in each group. The mean ages for the children were 5-3 (range 5-0 to 5-9) and 8-1 (range 7-1 to 9-0). The younger group consisted of nine girls and seven boys and was drawn from the same preschool as the subjects in Study 11. The older children consisted of eight girls and eight boys attending science camps or other summer programs. These children were also of largely upper-middle-class backgrounds.

Procedure

Prior to the administration of the basic tasks, subjects received lengthy pretraining. In the pretraining the second experimenter (E2) was initially asked questions about an absent object. Following her responses, the child was asked a similar set of questions and given feedback. This cycle was then repeated for objects present in the room.

The first experimenter (E1) began by saying, "See this flashlight. When it is working, it shines on some things but not on others. [The light was shone around the testing table.] Right now it is shining on my chin, but it is not shining on my nose. Now it is shining on Ellie's [E2's] mouth, but it is not shining on her chin. Your brain or mind is sort of like a flashlight. It shines on just a few things at a time, and while it shines on some things, it can't shine on others. I'll explain a bit more."

E2 was then asked to identify her favorite flavor of ice cream. She said, "Hmmm . . . chocolate." She was asked to move to a different chair, and a test question was given: "When you were sitting over there [E1 pointed], was your mind shining on anything?" E2 responded, "Yes, my mind was shining on ice cream. First it was shining on vanilla ice cream, and then on peppermint ice cream, and then chocolate. I thought about all those kinds of ice cream. But I like chocolate best." E1 restated what E2 had just said and asked about an irrelevant object: "OK. So your mind was shining on those different ice cream flavors. You were thinking about ice cream. While you were sitting over there [points again], did your mind also shine on your favorite movie?" E2 denied this, saying, "No, my mind wasn't shining on movies at all. I wasn't thinking about movies."

Both E2 and the subject were then asked to hold cassette tape covers, and E1 asked the child, "Of all your toys, which is your favorite?" The child was then moved to a new location and asked to put the tape cover down on the table. The subject was then asked about whether he or she had just been holding something, and, if so, what, and whether his or her mind had been shining on anything. If the response to the latter question was "yes," E1 asked, "What was your mind shining on?" If the child failed to mention anything related to toys, she probed further by asking, "Was your mind shining on anything else?" She continued to probe until the child responded "no." Feedback was then given as follows: "That's right/Actually your mind was shining on your toys. You were thinking about which toy was your favorite." The child was then asked if his or her mind had also been shining on an irrelevant topic, his or her best friends, and then given feedback: "That's right/Actually you weren't thinking about your best friends. Your mind wasn't shining on them."

The whole series of questions was repeated with objects present in the room. E1 first displayed a ring she was wearing: "Ellie, my husband gave me this ring." E2 said simply, "It's pretty." E2 was then asked to move and questioned about whether her mind had been shining on anything. She replied, "Yes, my mind was shining on your ring. I noticed it was blue." Then she was questioned about the tape recorder, an irrelevant object, and responded, "No. My mind wasn't shining on the tape recorder. I wasn't thinking about the tape recorder."

The child and E2 were then given small cans to hold, and a stuffed animal was shown to the child. "Here is a funny moose someone gave me. He is wearing glasses and skis." The child was asked to put the can down and to change locations. The pattern of questioning was just as mentioned above with respect to asking about what object had been held and whether the child's mind had been shining on anything while in the other location. Both the moose and the two cans were directly in front of the subject while these two questions were asked. The feedback given was, "That's right/ Actually you were thinking about that moose. Your mind was shining on that moose. You noticed what he was wearing." The child was then asked about an irrelevant object, the rug in the testing room. Following the response, E2 said, "That's right/Actually you weren't thinking about that rug. Your mind wasn't shining on it."

The three tasks described in Study 11 were then given. As in Study 11 also, experimenter feedback and modeling were provided between the first and the second tasks. The basic test question asked was, "While you were sitting over there in that other chair [points], was your mind shining on anything? Were you thinking about anything?" If the child responded affirmatively and gave content, the probe "Was your mind shining on anything else?" was continued until the response was "no." As before, subjects were tested for recognition of individual stimuli not previously mentioned, and the question format was identical to that used in Study 11, for example, ". . . Were you thinking about this x?" At the very end of the procedure those subjects who denied that they had been thinking about their bathroom were asked if they had been thinking about their toothbrush.

Results and Discussion

Subjects' responses to the initial, open-ended thinking questions were assigned to the categories "target," "other," and "none," exactly as in Study 11. Table 13, the counterpart in this study to Table 11 of Study 11 above, shows the percentage of children in each age group scored for each of these three categories (mental events) and the percentages correctly recalling what object they had held in their hand (physical events). The comparable data from Study 11 are included in parentheses. The 5-year-olds' performance is first examined and compared with that of the 5-year-olds in Study 11 and then compared to that of the 7–8-year-olds in this study.

Despite the more extensive pretraining and the provision of the flashlight analogy for mental attention, the 5-year-olds in this study were no

TABLE 13

Percentage Recall of Mental and Physical
Events in Study 12

Age and Task	Mental Events			Physical Events
	Target	Other	None	
5:				
Crayon	38	56	6	63
	(19)	(38)	(44)	(50)
Soap	38	56	6	69
	(13)	(44)	(44)	(63)
Bathroom	0	81	19	88
	(31)	(6)	(63)	(88)
7–8:				
Crayon	75	13	13	94
Soap	88	6	6	94
Bathroom	81	6	13	100

Note.—The figures in parentheses are the comparable percentages from Study 11
(see Table 11).

better at recalling their previous thoughts than the 5-year-olds in the previous study (cf. the leftmost columns of Tables 11 and 13). The numbers of subjects in this study correctly reporting target thoughts on three, two, one, and none of the three tasks were none, three, five, and eight, respectively; the corresponding numbers in Study 11 were none, three, four, and nine. Reports of target thoughts were more frequent this time on the Crayon (six vs. three) and Soap (six vs. two) tasks but less frequent on the Bathroom task—in fact, totally absent (none vs. five).

The main difference between the two sets of results was an increase from Study 11 to Study 12 in children's reports of other, nontarget thoughts (the category "other") and a corresponding decrease in failures to report any thoughts (the category "none") (cf. the second and third columns of Tables 11 and 13). Reports scored as "other" were often reported thoughts about the other objects that had been present while they were in the other chair and were now visible on the table in front of them: the two decoy objects (hidden, irrelevant) plus the object they had been holding in their hand. This was especially true on the Bathroom task, in which, remarkably, while none of the 13 subjects who said that they had been thinking said that they had thought either a bathroom or a toothbrush, eight said that they had thought about the pencil they had been holding.

Our interpretation is that the extensive pretraining increased their disposition to say that they had been thinking but not their ability to recall or reconstruct exactly what they had been thinking about. That is, the pretraining may have promoted affirmative responses without promoting any additional understanding of thinking about or enhancing their ability to retrieve previous thoughts. Level of recall of physical events was similar to that in Study 11: not really high but nearly significantly higher than recall of target mental events. Of the 16 subjects, 12 recalled a higher percentage of physical events than (target) mental events, and four showed the reverse pattern ($p < .08$, by Sign test). Again, this suggests that general memory limitations could not wholly account for 5-year-olds' problems in recalling their recent thoughts.

Table 14 shows the percentages of subjects correctly recognizing that they had thought about the targets, had not thought about the hidden and irrelevant decoy objects, and had held the specified objects while seated in the other chair. With the inexplicable exception of the hidden-object decoy in the Soap task, the children were again at least fairly good at recognizing that they had not thought about the decoy objects while in the chair. Recognition that they had thought about the target objects showed a nonsignificant increase from an average of 66% in Study 11 to an average of 74% in this study. At the end of the testing session the eight subjects who failed to recognize that they had thought of a bathroom were asked if they had thought about a toothbrush. All eight denied that they had. As in Study 11, the percentages of subjects who recognized both that they had thought about the two targets and that they had not thought about either decoy (the "All" column of Table 14) were quite low: means of 40% for Study 11 and 36% for this study.

Consistent with the recognition results of Study 11, mean recognition of previous physical events (100%) was perfect and significantly better than mean recognition of previous mental events (74%) ($t[15] = 4.39$, $p < .001$). As in Study 11 also, E2's modeling of correct responding after the first task proved to be of no significant help to the children on the second task, and

TABLE 14

PERCENTAGE CORRECT RECOGNITION/REJECTION OF MENTAL AND PHYSICAL
EVENTS IN STUDY 12

	MENTAL EVENTS					PHYSICAL EVENTS
AGE AND TASK	Target 1	Target 2	Hidden	Irrelevant	All	
5:						
Crayon	88	75	75	75	44	100
Soap	100	56	31	81	25	100
Bathroom	50	...	75	88	38	100
7–8:						
Crayon	100	88	100	94	81	100
Soap	100	100	100	100	100	100
Bathroom	94	...	100	100	94	100

a common recognition error on the Crayon and the Soap tasks was to report having thought about only the longer crayon or the real soap, that is, the correct choice or product of the thought process. In summary, the results of this study largely replicate those of Study 11 in showing that 5-year-olds have very limited ability to report accurately what they had recently been thinking about, even with the provision of considerable pretraining, practice trials with corrective feedback, experimenter modeling of correct responses, and what appeared to be a trio of very easy mental event retrospection tasks.

Tables 13 and 14 show clearly that the 7–8-year-olds performed considerably better than the 5-year-olds on all measures. Subjects were given scores of 0–3 depending on the number of tasks in which their mental event recall was categorized as "target." The scores of the older children were significantly higher than those of the younger ones ($t[29] = 5.52$, $p <$ .001). On the recognition measures, likewise, the older subjects' recognition of what they had and had not thought about was virtually perfect. Significantly, the group differences were apparent even during the pretraining period. For example, the percentages of the older subjects who said correctly that their minds had been shining on their toys in the first practice trial and on the funny moose in the second practice trial were 69% and 81%, respectively, whereas the corresponding percentages in the younger group were 31% and 25%. There were also qualitative differences between the groups in what they reported having thought about. The younger ones usually just listed or pointed to individual objects. In contrast, the older ones often said that they had been thinking about the problem or question posed to them. Examples are "Wondering which was real and if I was right or wrong" (Soap), "Which crayon was longer" (Crayon), "The question you asked me," "About the answer" (Bathroom).

We believe that the inclusion of the older group in this study proved to be useful in two ways. First, the dramatically better performance of this group suggests that children's introspective/retrospective abilities and associated knowledge about thinking may undergo important developments between 5 and 7 or 8 years. We examine this possibility further in Study 13. Second, the older subjects' good performance on all parts of all tasks suggests that these tasks were at least fairly clear, reasonable, and child friendly tests of the introspective abilities under study. To the extent that this is true, then the younger children's poor performance on them would reflect their poor introspective abilities, and also, perhaps, their limited understanding of focused mental attention, rather than the tasks' insensitivities as assessment devices. Of course we cannot be positive that the tasks were appropriate for younger children just because they proved suitable for older ones, but it seems a reasonable conclusion in the present case.

STUDY 13

Study 13 differed from the previous two in five ways. First, it was designed to give the child several different and interesting things to think about, things that should encourage rumination. Perhaps one reason that 5-year-olds did not perform better in Studies 11 and 12 was that the thought content engendered by our tasks was too brief and not sufficiently engaging. It may have been hard for them to remember or reconstruct their previous ideation because the problems posed did not have any lasting interest and did not encourage continued thought. Our hope was that at least one of the three objects shown on each task in this study would spark the child's curiosity. Second, objects were presented simply as "interesting things" rather than as decision problems, thereby avoiding the possible equation of *thinking about* with *the one I chose*.

Third, objects were not in view when the questions were asked and therefore could not be used as prompts for an implicit definition of *thinking* as "this is what I saw." Fourth, the content of the child's thought at the time the objects were presented was not queried, as it had been in the previous two studies. Rather, we asked the child about thought content occurring subsequent to the presentation of the materials, while the child is sitting in a different location. We did this in a further attempt to prevent children from thinking that their task was simply to recall the stimuli they had been shown. Finally, we did no pretraining in this study since we thought— possibly incorrectly, as the results later suggested—that the meaning of *thinking about* would be clear in context.

On each of two tasks we demonstrated to 5-year-old and 7–8-year-old children three objects chosen to be of interest or "thoughtworthy." Two magic tricks and one "problem" were included in each task. At the end of the testing session we administered a task designed to assess children's ability to monitor and report their thoughts on line, as they occurred. In this task, each child was instructed to say "teeth" whenever any of a series of 10 objects displayed made him or her think of teeth.

Method

Subjects

Two groups of children were tested, with 16 subjects in each group. The mean ages for the children were 5-3 (range 5-0 to 5-9) and 7-9 (range 7-0 to 8-11). The younger group, consisting of eight girls and eight boys, attended the same preschool as the 5-year-olds in Studies 11 and 12. The older group, consisting of six girls and 10 boys, attended either a summer science camp or a day camp. As in the previous studies, both groups were from primarily upper-middle-class backgrounds.

Procedure

The experimenter began by saying, "I've got some interesting things to show you." There followed two tasks, in counterbalanced order; the three objects in each task were always shown in the same order. In Task 1 the order was scarves, magic book, and pear, in Task 2 magic cups, candy, and light bulb. The magic tricks in Task 1 were as follows: two attached yellow and green scarves appeared to change to red and blue; identical pictures in a magic book seemed to change from full color to black and white. The "problem" was a narrow-necked bottle with a large pear inside it. In Task 2 the magic tricks were three cups with a ball that appeared to go through the bottoms of the cups and a light bulb that lit when it was held in the experimenter's hand and then seemed to be turned off by her blowing on it. The "problem" included two realistic-looking chocolate candies, one of which was actual chocolate, the other fake. The child was told that only one of the candies was real. The procedure is illustrated for Task 1.

The experimenter said, "Here are some special scarves. Yellow and green. Watch. [She pulled the scarves through her right hand.] My goodness. The yellow and green scarves disappeared. [Slight pause.] This is a magic book. [She riffled through the book.] Look at the pretty colored pictures. [She riffled again through the book.] Now they are in black and white. Strange. [Slight pause.] And here is a very large pear that somehow got into this little bottle. Hmmm. [Slight pause.] Well, we can look at these things again in just a few seconds. How about moving over to this chair for a little while while I get ready." The child moved to a new chair on another side of the table. The experimenter avoided eye contact with the child for 15 sec, then began the recall question. "While you have been sitting here in this chair [points], have you been thinking about anything or not?" If the child responded "yes," she said, "What have you been thinking about? Have you been thinking about anything else?" This probe continued until the reply was "no."

Next, the experimenter asked a series of recognition questions about each of the three test stimuli the child had not mentioned spontaneously. The questions were of the form, "While you have been sitting here [points], have you been thinking about the x or not?" As a partial control for a "yes" bias, she also asked about two objects (decoys) that the child, in all probability, had not been thinking about, the table (in view) and the moon (not in view). The decoys in Task 2 were the experimenter's chair and a fire engine. The recognition questions were asked in randomized orders for each subject.

After the recognition questions on each task, the major tricks were again demonstrated, with no explanation, the fake candy was unmasked, and the method of getting the pear into the bottle was explained (the bottle was put over it while it was still small so that it could grow inside the bottle). Prior to the child's second task, the experimenter said, "Now we'll do that same thing again. I have three more things to show you." Most children seemed to find the stimuli presented in these two tasks quite engaging. They frequently giggled and made comments about them, for example, "How did you do that?"

After the first two tasks, the experimenter said, "We'll try something now that we haven't done before. I will show you some different things, but I will not show you any teeth. You will not *see* any teeth. But maybe you will see something that will make you *think* about teeth, and maybe you won't. If you do happen to think about teeth, your job is to say 'teeth' out loud every time you think about them. When are you supposed to say 'teeth'?" If the child was unable to answer this question, the statement about his job was repeated, and then the question was repeated, until he or she answered correctly. The experimenter continued, "That's right, if you happen to think about teeth, say 'teeth.' But if you don't think about teeth, don't say 'teeth.'" Ten small objects were briefly shown, in a fixed order, from behind a screen: a small Snoopy, a toothbrush, a toy tricycle, a fake ear of corn, a dollhouse chair, a tube of toothpaste, a fork, dark glasses, a small lion, and a fake apple.

Results and Discussion

In this study, unlike the previous two, the task stimuli were no longer present during the 15-sec no-activity period for which introspections were solicited, with the result that we obviously could not be sure that all the children had in fact thought about the stimuli during this period. We therefore defined a more liberal "relevant" category that included not only references to the magic tricks and problems (the "target" category of Studies 11 and 12) but also anything else that seemed relevant or plausible. Examples of the latter included such responses as, "Why that said VOR" (the child had in fact asked this question about a tape recorder during the no-activity period), and, "What are you going to do next?" Most responses scored as "relevant" did consist of target responses, however. The categories "other" and "none" were scored as in the two previous studies. Only 5-year-olds gave any "other" responses in this study. Examples are, "Your chair," "My brother," and, "Getting a water gun." While it is certainly possible that they actually were thinking of such things right after having seen the magic tricks and problems, it did not seem very likely—especially since the older children did not report any such off-task thoughts.

Table 15 shows the percentages of 5- and 7–8-year-olds scored for each of these three categories in Tasks 1 and 2. Consistent with the results of Study 12, the older subjects recalled significantly more relevant thought content than the younger ones did (for Task 1, $\chi^2[2] = 10.24$, $p < .01$; for Task 2, $\chi^2[2] = 10.49$, $p < .01$). Although obviously much higher than that of the 5-year-olds, the level of recall of the 7–8-year-olds was nevertheless not very high in absolute terms (mean = 63%). One might have expected that the recognition tests on their first task would have given subjects a helpful hint as to what they might have been thinking about (namely, one or more of the three surprising or puzzling stimuli), thereby leading them to increase their relevant recall on their second task. This did not happen with either age group, however: recall levels were substantially the same on both tasks. One possible explanation for the relatively low level of relevant recall is that, despite what we hoped would happen, a number of subjects did in fact stop thinking about the stimuli after they had been removed and also had no other thoughts salient enough for them to recall easily. It may also have been the case that the absence of pretraining in this study made for a lesser sensitivity to the presence of thinking in general, for both age groups.

The recognition data shown in Table 16 lend some support to the above explanation. Recall that, in Study 12, 7–8-year-olds' recognition scores were very high (Table 14 above), suggesting that children of this age can accurately recognize what they have and have not recently thought about in simple situations such as these. In contrast, the recognition scores shown in Table 16 by same-aged children are considerably lower. This suggests that a number of these children may have been correctly reporting that

TABLE 15

PERCENTAGE RECALL OF MENTAL
EVENTS IN STUDY 13

	MENTAL EVENTS		
AGE AND TASK	Relevant	Other	None
5:			
1	6	25	69
2	13	19	69
7–8:			
1	56	0	44
2	69	0	31

TABLE 16

Percentage Correct Recognition/Rejection of Mental Events in Study 13

	MENTAL EVENTS				
AGE AND TASK	Target 1	Target 2	Target 3	Decoy 1	Decoy 2
5:					
1	75	63	56	63	69
2	63	44	75	81	69
7–8:					
1	56	69	69	88	88
2	75	69	69	94	94

they had not thought about our stimuli during the 15-sec period following their removal. Interestingly, it can be seen in Table 16 that the recognition scores in the present study for the 5-year-olds (mean = 63%) are very similar to those of the 7–8-year-olds (mean = 68%), although their recall scores are much lower. Although it may be the case that the younger subjects recall fewer Relevant thoughts than the older ones because they had fewer to recall (i.e., they really did think about the stimuli less), the fact that their recognition scores were as high as the older subjects' does not encourage this interpretation. Rather, it seems more likely to us that, as in Study 12, the younger children were simply poorer than the older ones at recalling or reconstructing their recent mental content.

On their final task subjects were asked to say "teeth" each time they saw something that made them think about teeth. They were then presented with a series of 10 objects, five that seemed more likely to trigger this association (toothbrush, ear of corn, toothpaste, fork, apple), and five that seemed less likely to do so (Snoopy, tricycle, chair, dark glasses, lion). Subjects in both groups seldom (none or one subject per group) said "teeth" when they saw any of the supposed nonassociated items; consequently, almost all such reports were in response to the intended associated items. The older subjects said "teeth" significantly more often than the younger ones ($t[26] = 2.28, p < .05$). They did so on 65% of the associated items, younger subjects doing so on only 36%. Likewise, eight of the younger children never made this response, whereas only one older child never did ($p < .05$, by Fisher's exact test).

These results suggest to us that 5-year-olds are probably poorer than 7–8-year-olds at noticing current thoughts as well as poorer at recalling or reconstructing recent ones. On the other hand, at least two other, alternative interpretations cannot be ruled out: (*a*) that fewer of the younger children were able to adopt or maintain the set to monitor their consciousness for the occurrence of the target thought; (*b*) that the associated objects triggered this thought less often in the younger subjects than in the older ones. One of the objectives of Study 14 was to provide an additional test of younger children's ability to notice and report their current thoughts.

STUDY 14

The main objective of this study was to provide the easiest context we could imagine to assist young children in reporting their thinking. One way in which we tried to simplify task demands was to ask subjects about their current thinking and to do so right after presenting a thought-provoking stimulus. Two stories that violated expectations and two unusual objects were presented to 5-year-old children. Following each presentation and a 1–2-sec delay, subjects were asked whether they were currently wondering about or thinking about anything. Unlike Studies 11–13, this study did not include recognition tests. In a fifth task, always given last, subjects learned to expect the experimenter to ring a bell after a short delay. When she unexpectedly failed to do so after a much longer delay, the same test question was asked. In addition to probing for current rather than previous thinking and adding the potentially helpful word *wondering* to the test question, we provided brief pretraining in hopes of getting the subject to focus on the process of thinking rather than the product or solution. We did not want children to deny that they were thinking just because they did not have a way to explain the objects or stories presented to them.

Method

Subjects

Sixteen 5-year-olds were tested. The mean age for the group was 5-4 (range 5-0 to 6-0). The group consisted of eight boys and eight girls. A few of the children attended the laboratory preschool mentioned previously. The rest attended either a kindergarten in a private school or an after-school program at a nearby elementary school. All the children were of upper-middle-class backgrounds.

Procedure

Brief pretraining was conducted as follows. The experimenter said, "Before we start I want to explain something. You know sometimes when we think about problems we *can* figure out the answers. Like yesterday—my keys weren't in my purse. I tried to figure out where I had put them, and I did—I remembered they were in my pocket. But sometimes when we think about problems, even if we think very hard, we *cannot* figure out the answers. Like this morning I tried to figure out who went to the circus with me last year. But even though I couldn't remember I was still wondering and thinking about who went with me. In the game today I will tell you some unusual stories and show you some unusual objects. Then I will ask you a few questions." The tasks were blocked by task type, with the stories given as one block, the objects as another. These blocks were counterbalanced across subjects. Within each block were two tasks with a control task inserted between them. The positions of these two tasks were also counterbalanced.

Objects.—The pear in the bottle and the magic cups from Study 13 were the two stimuli for these tasks. The experimenter introduced the pear by saying, "Here is something unusual. There's a pretty big pear in there. But look, this opening at the top is very little. Hmmm." The pear was removed from sight, and after a 1–2-sec delay the basic test question was asked: "Are you wondering about or thinking about anything right now or not?" If the answer was "yes," the experimenter asked, "What are you wondering or thinking about?" In some instances, rather than responding "yes" or "no" to the open-ended question, the child either asked the experimenter a question or offered a solution to the problem. In these instances, the experimenter asked, "Is that what you were wondering or thinking about?"

For the magic cups, she said, "Here are some magic cups. Here is a little ball." She turned the three cups upside down and then said, "Now when you look at these cups, you can see there are no holes in the bottom. Watch what I can do." She next stacked up the cups, the bottom one containing the hidden ball. On top of the second cup she placed the ball the subject knew about, then covered that ball with a third cup. She continued, "Abracadabra. Look at that. There's the ball [under the bottom cup]. Hmmm." The cups were removed and the test questions asked as previously described. The control task, in which we expected the child to be less likely to say "yes" to the test question, drew the child's attention to the experimenter's eyeglasses before the test questions were administered. The experimenter said, "These are the glasses I bought a little while ago. They help me see much better."

Stories.—One story was as follows: "Susan was very hungry when she got home from school. She decided to have cereal with milk on top. She likes shredded wheat, so she put some of that in a bowl. She took the milk carton from the refrigerator and started to pour the contents over her cereal. Only large clumps of dirt came out of the milk carton. Ugh. Susan was really surprised. Hmmm." The second story was as follows: "A man and his wife decided to go to the same store. The wife decided to drive their car. The man decided to walk. But the man got to the store faster. I thought cars were faster than walking. Somehow the man got there first.

Hmmm." The innocuous control story was as follows: "The other day I went to the pet food store and bought my cats lots of food. Do you like cats? I like cats too." The test question(s) followed each of these three stories.

A *Bell* task was given at the end of the testing session. We intended this task as a converging measure to the main tasks previously described as it also involved violated expectations. The experimenter showed the child a library-type bell and then hid it under the testing table. She said, "In just a few seconds I'll ring it." After a 4-sec delay she rang the bell and said, "OK, in just a few seconds I'll ring it again." After another 4-sec delay she rang the bell and reiterated, "OK, one more time. In just a few seconds I'll ring it again." This time she failed to ring the bell and after a 10–12-sec delay instead asked the same test question(s) previously described. Following this task she explained to the child how the pear got into the bottle.

Results and Discussion

As in Study 13, relevant responses included references to the task stimuli or any other content that seemed relevant or plausible (the latter were rare). Examples of responses scored "relevant" are, "The pear in the wine bottle" (Pear), "How did the dirt get in there?" (Dirt), "I am sort of wondering about what you are going to say in the story" (Control 1), and, "Wondering when you are going to ring that thing" (Bell). The categories "other" and "none" were scored as in Studies 11–13. Table 17 shows the percentages of children scored for each of these categories on each of the seven tasks.

The table shows that 5-year-olds performed better on the Pear, Cups, Dirt, and Store tasks in this study than on comparable tasks in Studies 11, 12, and 13 (see the "Target" columns in Tables 11 and 13 above and the "Relevant" column in Table 15 above). For example, six of the 16 children gave "relevant" responses on all four of these tasks, and three more did so on three of the four tasks. In addition, the virtual absence of "other" responses shows that almost all reported thought content was situation appropriate. (Recall that 5-year-olds also performed quite well on the one-trial

TABLE 17

PERCENTAGE RECALL OF MENTAL EVENTS IN STUDY 14

	TASK						
RESPONSE	Pear	Cups	Dirt	Store	Control 1	Control 2	Bell
Relevant	75	63	56	56	38	38	38
Other	6	0	6	6	0	6	19
None	19	38	38	38	63	56	44

introspection posttest of Study 10, described at the end of the previous chapter.)

It could be argued, however, that these data may overestimate somewhat the group's actual introspective ability. In some cases children were clearly intending to tell us what they had been thinking, for example, "Thinking about how you did that." In other cases, however, they may have simply been asking the experimenter a question (e.g., "How did you do that?") or making a comment (e.g., "I think he was not really walking"), without thinking of what they were saying as a report of their own thoughts. In support of this interpretation, two children offered solutions to the Store problem before the experimenter could ask the test question ("Maybe he ran," one of them volunteered), but then said "no" when asked, "Is that what you were wondering or thinking about?"

In addition, it should be noted in Table 17 that subjects denied thinking or wondering about anything at all on 19%–38% of the tasks. The lower percentage of relevant responses on the Bell task (38%, the same as on the two control tasks) is more consistent with the results of the three prior introspection studies and also suggests caution in interpreting the Pear, Cups, Dirt, and Store results. One would think that all the children must have been wondering why the bell did not ring as expected on the Bell task, yet only five of the 16 subjects reported having wondered that.

The results of this study, then, do not appreciably alter the conclusion drawn from the preceding three. Five-year-olds have quite poor introspective skills, with the result that they are apt to perform poorly even on very easy-seeming introspection tasks.

CONCLUSIONS ABOUT PRESCHOOLERS' INTROSPECTION SKILLS

Farthing (1992) distinguishes two types of consciousness: *primary* and *reflective*. Primary consciousness is the direct experience of percepts, feelings, thoughts, memories, and the like. Animals and human infants have primary consciousness, at least for percepts and feelings. Reflective consciousness consists of thoughts and awareness concerning these experiences, with the reflected-on experiences being thought of as mental events. Thus, whereas primary consciousness is a form of cognition, reflective consciousness is a form of metacognition. Introspection is an instance of reflective consciousness because it consists of reflecting on, and perhaps also verbally reporting on, primary-conscious mental events construed as mental events by the reflecting person.

How much skill at introspection did preschoolers show in the very simple introspection tasks described in this chapter? We can identify four levels of response to these tasks:

1. Although the nature of the task ensured that the subject had in fact been thinking during the time period under inquiry, when asked, he or she does not report having done any thinking.

2. The subject errs by reporting thoughts that either certainly or almost certainly had not occurred during this period.

3. The subject accurately reports objects or events that he or she had in fact been thinking about, for example, "the crayons" or "this one" (the real soap) in Studies 11 and 12. However, the report is construed by the subject as a factual report of the external objects or events encountered during this period or something similar, rather than as an introspective, reflective consciousness–type report of thoughts concerning them.

4. Level 4 is the same as level 3, with the crucial difference that the subject thinks of what he or she is doing as reporting mental activity concerning the task objects and events rather than as just reporting the presence of the objects and events themselves. Thus, level 4 is genuine introspection, whereas level 3 is not. The distinction is important. For example, we would not want to claim that a 2-year-old who reports some fact that she suddenly remembered was introspecting when she did so. The reason is that she was undoubtedly thinking only of the objective fact itself, not about the subjective event or the experience of remembering it.

Inspection of Tables 11, 13, 15, and 17 shows that preschoolers displayed very limited introspection skills on our tasks. Most of their many responses classified as "none" or "other" represent clear-cut failures to introspect successfully, being instances of levels 1 and 2, respectively. Furthermore, how many of their correct reports (those scored as "target" or "relevant") were actually instances of level 4 and how many of level 3 is unknown. As already indicated, however, it often appeared that subjects were just reporting something about the target objects and events themselves (level 3) rather than trying to recall their own inner, mental reactions to them (level 4, or genuine introspection).

Although we did not administer these tasks to adult subjects in these studies, it is hard to imagine that they would not have found them extremely easy; they were, after all, the easiest-seeming introspection tasks that we, also adults, were able to devise. Although adults may have limited introspective access to the exact causes of their recent conscious thoughts (Nisbett & Wilson, 1977), the research evidence indicates that they can usually describe the thoughts themselves with considerable accuracy (Ericsson & Simon, 1993; Farthing, 1992). Merely recognizing in Studies 11 and 12 that they had just been trying to decide which of two crayons was the longer would surely have been easier than reporting the sequence of mental steps that they had just taken in solving some problem—an introspection task they routinely perform successfully in adult verbal report studies (Ericsson & Simon, 1993). Moreover, given the clear instructions to introspect, they would surely also have been aware that it was their thinking about the crayons and not the crayons themselves that they were trying to recall. Indeed, the 7–8-year-olds in Studies 12 and 13 also performed quite well on our introspection tasks, although undoubtedly less well than adults would have (see Table 15 above).

We conclude, therefore, that preschoolers have very limited introspective skills compared with adults, if one accepts the usual definition of *introspection* as the attempted recall of mental events coupled with the awareness that it is mental rather than physical events that are being sought. It appears from our data that these skills undergo considerable improvement during the early elementary school years, but when they approximate those of adults must remain a question for future research. We also do not know what situations facilitate the use of whatever introspective skills young children do possess, although some ideas about this are proposed at the end of the next chapter.

V. CONCLUSIONS

In the previous chapters we have reported 14 studies assessing young children's knowledge about *thinking* or *mental attention,* defined broadly to include even minimal mental contact with some content. In this chapter we draw on the results of these and other studies to offer five sets of conclusions. First, we summarize what preschoolers (3–5-year-olds) already appear to know about thinking. Second, we cite a number of things that they appear not to know about it, or at least not to know very well.[3] Third, we try to specify more precisely the underlying system of knowledge about thinking that they lack and will subsequently need to acquire. Fourth, we suggest some possible implications of the foregoing for children's everyday thought and behavior. Finally, we speculate about experiential factors that might impede or facilitate their acquisition of additional knowledge about thinking.

WHAT PRESCHOOLERS KNOW ABOUT THINKING

1. Preschoolers seem to realize that thinking is something that only people and perhaps some other animates engage in. When Dolgin and Behrend (1984) asked subjects of different ages which of a series of animate and inanimate objects "can think," they found that even 3- and 4-year-olds understood that people can think and inanimates cannot. Although our preschool subjects often failed to attribute thinking to themselves and others when they should have, there was no suggestion that any subject doubted that thinking was something that people could and did do.

2. They recognize that thinking is some kind of internal, mental event

---

[3] It should be remembered that our subjects were mostly American children of primarily upper-middle-class backgrounds. Whether children of other socioeconomic backgrounds or from other cultures would respond as ours did obviously cannot be known without further research.

or process. As indicated in Chapter I, Wellman and his coworkers (Estes et al., 1989; Wellman, 1990; Wellman & Estes, 1986; Woolley & Wellman, 1992, 1993) have shown that preschoolers distinguish between mental and physical entities. For example, they understand that, unlike a real, external object, an imaged or thought-of or dreamed-of object is not a physical, public, and tangible entity. Moreover, they can form images deliberately on request, seemingly recognizing that the request is to do something co-vert—in their head—rather than overt.

Johnson and Wellman's (1982) finding that 4- and 5-year-olds tend to believe that one thinks with one's brain and that the brain is inside the head also suggests that they construe thinking as an internal, in-the-head affair. All our observations suggest this same conclusion. Our subjects did not behave as if they believed that thinking was some sort of overt act or that people who were not acting overtly could therefore not be thinking. They never mistakenly proffered overt actions when asked to think (in some of the pretests), nor did they ever seem perplexed when an experimenter who was performing no overt action said that she was thinking. Although they sometimes used expressive behavior (e.g., a thoughtful expression) as a clue to thinking, there was no suggestion that they believed that thinking actually *was* that expressive behavior. As will be seen, there is much that preschoolers appear not to understand about thinking, but they do at least seem to under-stand that it is some sort of internal happening.

3. Preschoolers realize that, like desires and other mental entities, think-ing has content and makes reference. They know that, when people think, they think of or about something. They recognize that the object of thought need not be physically present (e.g., Study 2); indeed, they know that it need not even really exist anywhere outside the thinker's imagination (e.g., the aforementioned studies by Wellman and his colleagues).

Combining claims 1–3, we conclude that preschoolers have at least a minimal grasp of the bare-bones essentials of thinking: namely, that it is some sort of internal, mental activity that people engage in that refers to real or imaginary objects or events. In view of the research evidence that children of this age already know something about mental states such as desires and beliefs, it is not surprising that they understand this much about thinking.

4. They distinguish thinking from other activities or states that com-monly accompany it and with which they might understandably confuse it. They realize that a person who cannot see something could nevertheless be thinking about it (Studies 2, 3); this finding is also consistent with the claim (point 3 above) that preschoolers believe that one can think about absent objects. Similarly, they understand that a person who is not currently per-forming the overt actions of talking about or touching something may nev-ertheless be thinking about it (Study 3); this finding further supports the

claim (point 2 above) that preschoolers construe thinking as a covert action or event. Study 1 also provided some weaker evidence in support of an early seeing-thinking and action-thinking differentiation.

Although their understanding of knowing, like that of thinking itself, is still quite hazy at this age (Lyon, 1993; Montgomery, 1992), the results of Studies 4–6 suggest that preschoolers can also distinguish thinking from knowing to some extent. For example, they seemed to recognize that one could still have knowledge of things about which one is not presently thinking. Finally, probably no one in this research area would hypothesize that children initially equate desiring or liking with thinking about because knowledge about desires develops quite early. Consistent with this consensus view, subjects in Studies 9 and 10 did not seem unwilling to say that the second experimenter (E2) was thinking about an object just because she did not like it, although they often had trouble inferring which objects she was and was not thinking about.

By distinguishing thinking from these other psychological processes or states, preschoolers give further evidence that they are beginning to understand at least roughly what it means to think of or about something.

5. Preschoolers have some ability to infer the presence of ongoing mental activity in another person from available evidence (Studies 3, 7, 8, 9, 10; Baron-Cohen & Cross, 1992; Flavell et al., 1993, study 1; Rosenkrantz, 1991). However, they tend to require very strong and clear evidence to do so and will not always do so even when such evidence is present. Here, as elsewhere, older preschoolers tend to display more competence than younger ones. The cues that can lead to this inference can apparently be either behavioral (the person looks reflective or agrees to take on some thinking task) or situational (the person is offered some thinking task or is in an emotionally arousing situation).

WHAT PRESCHOOLERS DO NOT KNOW ABOUT THINKING

Preschoolers are generally poor at determining both *when* a person (the self or another) is thinking and *what* the person is and is not thinking about. These and other conclusions are elaborated and documented below.

1. Preschoolers greatly underestimate the amount of mental activity that goes on in people. They do not realize that people are continually experiencing mental content of one kind or another—the ever-flowing "stream of consciousness" described by William James (1890, p. 239). In three studies, Flavell et al. (1993) showed that, unlike older subjects, preschoolers do not consistently attribute any mental activity to a person who just sits quietly, "waiting." They respond this way whether the presence of mental activity is described as the person "having some thoughts or ideas"

or, even more inclusively and nonspecifically, as the person's "mind doing something."

This conclusion was also supported by the results of Studies 7 and 8 of the present investigation. The Study 8 findings seem particularly compelling: even when 4-year-olds had the option of agreeing with an explicit statement of the unstoppable-stream-of-consciousness position ("something is always going on in people's minds, so there *must* be something going on" in a physically inactive experimenter's mind) rather than agreeing with an appearance-based option ("it doesn't *look like* anything is going on in her mind, so probably nothing is going on"), only 38% of the sample did so on both their two opportunities to make such a choice.

Also consistent with this conclusion was the finding in Flavell et al.'s (1993) second study that 4-year-olds seem less certain than adults are that a person would not be able to keep his or her mind completely empty of all thoughts and ideas for a prolonged period. Lacking any sort of stream-of-consciousness intuition, young children are probably forced to rely either on guesswork or on behavioral and situational cues to make positive attributions of mental activity.

2. Preschoolers also do not automatically assume that something must be "going on in a person's mind" or that the person's mind must be "doing something," even when that person is known to be engaged in the activities of looking at something (Studies 7 and 8), reading (Study 7), listening to something (Studies 7 and 8), talking to another person (Study 7), and, for a number of younger preschoolers at least, even deciding something (Study 7). They also do not consistently assume that they themselves must have been thinking while engaged with various thought-provoking stimuli or tasks (Studies 11–14). It is surprising enough that preschoolers are not aware that they and other people are experiencing one or another sort of cognitive content more or less continually, even when doing nothing in particular. However, it is more surprising to discover that they do not even seem to know that cognitive activities like looking, listening, reading, and talking necessarily entail such experiences.

3. Even when they do recognize that a person is thinking, preschoolers tend to be poor at inferring from the available evidence what the person is thinking about, even in situations where that evidence is very strong and compelling. The results of Study 7 showed that, on those occasions when they did attribute mental activity to a person who was reading or trying to make a decision, for example, they were often unable to make plausible inferences about the likely content of that activity. In Studies 11–14 they also frequently failed to identify accurately what they themselves had just recently been thinking about. They sometimes reported that they (Studies 11–13) or another person (Studies 4 and 6) had thought about objects that they or the other person clearly had not thought about, either instead of

or in addition to reporting what had actually been thought about. However, the most dramatic evidence for this difficulty was seen in Studies 9 and 10. In Study 9, E1 asked E2 a thought-provoking question about one of two objects present. E2 replied, "That's a hard question. Give me a minute. Hmmm." She then turned to one side and looked very pensive. Despite this strong evidence, preschoolers were surprisingly poor at choosing that object over the other one as the object E2 was currently thinking about. In Study 10, the evidence for the focus of her preoccupation was even stronger: she also faced, stared at, and occasionally touched the target object while looking reflective, rather than facing to one side. Despite this additional help, a number of younger preschoolers, especially, still failed to recognize consistently that she was thinking about the target object and was not thinking about the nontarget object.

4. Consistent with previous findings by Pillow (1988, 1989a), the results of Studies 4, 6, and 10 indicate that preschoolers tend to have a poor understanding of attentional focus and attentional limits. They do not seem to understand that, when one focuses one's thought and attention on one thing, one is not also thinking about other things. After having said that a person was currently thinking about one thing, preschoolers would often say that the person was also currently thinking about one or more other, even unrelated things. Similarly, in the "thought bubbles" posttest of Study 10, only the older subjects (5-year-olds) tended to say that a person who was thinking would have only one thought rather than many in his or her head during a very brief moment of time.

It is possible that preschoolers tend to conceive of thought or the mind as more akin to a lamp than a spotlight, that is, as something that can shine in many directions at once rather than in only one. Combining conclusions 3 and 4, when they do infer that a person is thinking, preschoolers are apt not to understand clearly that the thinking is at any given moment necessarily focused on only one object or topic rather than on a number of them and that one can often be predicted accurately from situational cues.

5. The aforementioned difficulties are also very evident when preschoolers deal with their own mental activity rather than another person's (see the concluding section of Chap. IV). As Studies 11–14 and Flavell et al.'s (1993) Study 3 clearly show, preschoolers tend to be very poor at recalling or reconstructing both the fact and the content of their own thinking, even in situations designed to facilitate introspection. In Studies 11 and 12, for example, 5-year-olds who at the experimenter's instigation had clearly just been thinking about which room in their house they keep their toothbrush in often denied that they had just been thinking; moreover, in those instances where they did say they had been thinking, they often did not mention either a toothbrush or a bathroom when asked what they had been thinking about. In contrast, subjects of 7 or 8 years of age proved to be

much better than 5-year-olds at such introspection tasks (Studies 12 and 13).

6. Preschoolers show little understanding of what Gordon and Flavell (1977) referred to as *cognitive cueing*, that is, the tendency of one mental event to trigger the occurrence of another mental event that is related to the first in some way in the thinker's experience (Cohen, 1993; Gordon & Flavell, 1977; Hansen, 1993; Schneider & Sodian, 1988; Sodian & Schneider, 1990). Adults show their awareness of cognition when they say such things as, "Oh, that reminds me," or, "You *would* have to say that—now I'll worry!"

To illustrate preschoolers' difficulties here, in a recent study (Cohen, 1993) conducted in our laboratory, 4-year-olds were presented with a picture story in which a child happens to think about beautiful flowers while at the beach. Later, she sees some beautiful flowers plus three other control objects and suddenly thinks about the beach. When asked what made her think about the beach, most of the 4-year-olds had no idea. They also did not consistently identify the flowers even when asked more directly which of the four objects "made her think of the beach."

Gordon and Flavell (1977), Hansen (1993), and Sodian and Schneider (1990) have shown that there is considerable development between 4 and 6 or 7 years in children's understanding of cognitive cueing. We have previously speculated that this development might be related to a growing awareness of the stream of consciousness:

> It seems possible that children's understanding of cognitive cueing and of the stream of consciousness might develop together, with each concept perhaps facilitating the acquisition of the other. On the one hand, as they become aware that they have first one thought, then another, then another in an extended sequence or stream, they might notice that one thought is often related semantically to, and seemingly stimulated by, its predecessor. Conversely, coming to realize that one thought often cues the next which often cues the next, and so on, leads naturally to the idea that there would be extended sequences or streams of such interlinked thoughts rather than just occasional islands of isolated thoughts with nothing between them. (Flavell et al., 1993, p. 397)

7. There are also suggestions in our data (suggestions only) that preschoolers may tend to equate mental activity with mental products rather than with the mental processes that generate them. That is, they may tend to identify thinking with the answer, solution, or stimulus selection eventually arrived at rather than with the mental efforts and activities that led up to them. Thus, in the first study of Flavell et al. (1993), some 4-year-olds were reluctant to attribute any thoughts and ideas to E2 on the problem-solving task because, although obviously thinking hard about the problem, she had

not yet solved it. In Studies 11 and 12, 5-year-olds would often deny having thought about the crayon that they had not judged to be the longer of the two, or the object that they had not judged to be the real soap, even though they showed by their eye movements that they had also considered these "nonsolution" objects.

In contrast, 7–8-year-olds usually mentioned having thought about both the chosen and the nonchosen object. They also sometimes alluded to an extended and uncompleted mental process rather than just indicating one of the objects ("the solution"), as the younger subjects usually did. For example, one older subject said, "Wondering which was real and if I was right or wrong." In Study 7 also, preschoolers sometimes focused only on which of the two objects they thought the story character in the Decide situation would choose, seemingly oblivious to the decision process that would generate that choice.

These observations are consistent with the widespread view in the field that children acquire an increasingly constructivist, process-oriented conception of the mind during middle childhood and adolescence (Chandler, 1988; Pillow, in press; Schwanenflugel, Fabricius, & Alexander, in press; Taylor, 1988; Wellman, 1990). They are also consistent with our belief (see the last section of Chap. IV) that our young subjects' introspective reports were often just disguised objective reports of the external objects and events that they had encountered. That is, even when they accurately reported the objects that they had thought about, they were construing these reports as reports about objects rather than as reports about thoughts of objects.

8. In future research we plan to test for other possible developments in this area. For example, we believe that, although young children probably realize that one can start thinking about something just by deciding to, they may not realize that one cannot always stop thinking about something just by deciding not to; thinking is partly controllable, but also partly uncontrollable (Wegner, Schneider, Carter, & White, 1987). The fact that one thought tends to trigger another (cognitive cueing) and that one cannot succeed in stopping the flow of one's stream of consciousness for long are instances of the partial uncontrollability of thought, and we already know that preschoolers are largely unaware of these facts.

Do young children realize that it can be hard to suppress scary thoughts or other types of persistent ideation? We also wonder whether they construe inner, covert speech as a form or vehicle of thinking. Indeed, we wonder how aware they are of the existence of inner speech; certainly, no indications of such awareness surfaced in any of our studies. Finally, we imagine that preschoolers might be quite hazy about the enormous difference between one's subjective experience when conscious and one's subjective experience when unconscious (dreaming experiences excepted). This would seem to follow from their apparent failure to envisage an increasing flow of inner experiences (the stream of consciousness) in conscious individuals. Developing some sense of what subjective experience is not like when one is unconscious may help them better appreciate what it is like when one is conscious.

A DEVELOPMENTAL HYPOTHESIS

The foregoing conclusions suggest a general hypothesis about how young children's and adults' conceptions of mental activity might differ and therefore about what children might need to learn about mental activity in order to be able to conceive of it the way we think most adults do. This hypothesis owes much to related ideas about children's developing understanding of the causes and effects of mental states proposed by Gopnik and Graf (1988), Leslie (1988), O'Neill, Astington, and Flavell (1992), O'Neill and Gopnik (1991), Pillow (1989b), Pratt and Bryant (1990), Wellman (1990), and Wimmer, Hogrefe, and Sodian (1988).

According to this hypothesis, adults tend to conceive of individual thoughts as being embedded in a whole network of potential psychological causes and effects. Thus, they understand that thoughts may be instigated by wholly internal events such as memories and feelings as well as by perceptions of external objects and events. They also realize that, once instigated, a thought will typically set in motion a train of related thoughts. Because they understand that the instigators can be of internal as well as external origin, they expect that trains of thought will occur even when the thinker is not attending to anything in the external environment. In addition, adults understand that thoughts commonly engender other mental states (beliefs, feelings, desires, intentions, etc.) and overt actions. Adults do not suppose that they can identify the causes and effects of all thoughts, and they may not even assume that all thoughts have causes and effects. Nevertheless, they do believe that thoughts often do have causes and effects, and they also know the general sorts of causes and effects that they may have.

Young children's conception of thoughts is quite different from that of adults, according to this hypothesis. First, the concept of a thought (thinking, mental activity, etc.) is doubtless less salient for them than it is for most adults; they do not think about thoughts very often spontaneously. When they are brought to think about them, however, they are more likely than adults to regard them as isolated and largely inexplicable mental happenings, not linked to preceding causes or subsequent effects. Although they may occasionally become aware that something instigated a thought (e.g., an instruction to think, an emotionally arousing situation) or that a thought instigated something (e.g., an action based on that thought), the question of possible causes and effects usually does not even arise for them when thinking about thinking.

If young children did tend to construe thoughts as isolated, mysterious mental events, largely uncaused and uncausing, it would help explain some of the curious limitations that preschoolers have shown in this and other investigations. Unaware of the myriad internal and external events that can trigger thoughts, and unaware of the chain-reaction-like flashings of whole sequences of thoughts, each cognitively cueing its successor, they greatly underestimate the sheer quantity of conscious mental content that people spontaneously experience. Not expecting mentation to be going on more or less continuously in people, they understandably require strong behavioral or situational evidence to infer its presence. Consequently, they are unlikely to feel sure that a perceptually and behaviorally inactive person who has been given no cognitive task—our "waiting" E2, for instance—is having "some thoughts and ideas," a mind that is "doing something," or the like. Having no causal theory that would lead them to do otherwise, they naturally tend to go only by appearance.

Furthermore, inattentive to causes of thoughts generally, they do not realize that perceptual input automatically sets into motion trains of thought. As a result, they do not consistently attribute mental activity even to a person whom they know to be presently engaged in looking, listening, or reading. Not usually thinking of thoughts as having perceptual or other causes, they do not automatically anticipate cognitive sequelae when given evidence only of perceptual activities. Even when they do infer the presence of thinking, because they are ignorant of cognitive cueing they will envisage only a few punctate, isolated thoughts rather than an extended thought *process* or Jamesian *stream* of thoughts. Not surprisingly, therefore, they do not have a constructivist, process-oriented conception of cognition in which the mind goes "beyond the information given" (Bruner, 1973) to create an elaborated interpretation of this information.

Just as the known presence of common causes of thoughts (e.g., percepts) does not reliably lead preschoolers to infer the presence of thoughts, so conversely does the inferred presence of thoughts not reliably lead them to look to those causes as clues to the content of those thoughts. Thus, for example, even when they do infer that a person who is reading something is thinking, they may not make the further inference that the person is thinking about whatever he or she is reading. Similarly, not understanding that the causes of thoughts constrain their contents, young children are more willing than their elders to allow that a person who is completely absorbed with one object could also be thinking about something wholly unrelated. To illustrate, in Studies 9 and 10 preschoolers often said that E2 was also or instead thinking about an object other than the one with which she was obviously preoccupied, that is, an object that she "had no cause" to be thinking about at that moment. For a child for whom the world of thought is largely causeless, any thought might occur at any time.

One would expect that children with this conception of thinking would also be poor at identifying the fact and content of their own thinking. Indeed, they would be at a triple disadvantage in our introspection tasks. First, when asked whether they had been thinking about anything just previously, they would not begin with the assumption that they must have been for the reason that people are always thinking about one thing or another. Second, not realizing that what they had experienced perceptually during the time period in question would automatically trigger thoughts semantically related to those perceptual experiences, they would be unable to reason backward to infer the probable contents of the thoughts from the remembered contents of the experiences. For example, they could not just recall that they had seen a baffling magic trick and then simply infer that seeing it would naturally have caused thoughts about it. Third, they could not go on to use these inferences as retrieval cues to trigger actual episodic memories of precisely what thoughts they had had.

Although differences in young children's and adults' understanding of the causal context of thinking may help explain preschoolers' performance on our tasks, they are undoubtedly not the only differences that exist. Other possible "developables" were cited in the last paragraph of the previous section (point 8). In addition, adults also undoubtedly know more than young children do about what thoughts are like, as well as knowing more about what can cause them and about what they can cause. Adults understand that thoughts can be of a wide variety of kinds and can have a wide variety of contents. They know that in our minds we imagine, assert, deny, question, compare, analyze, interpret, etc. all manner of things—complex or simple, factual or fanciful. Although additional evidence would be needed to confirm and specify age differences here, it seems very likely that young children still have much to learn about all the different sorts of thoughts that people have.

IMPLICATIONS

If young children had the limited understanding of thinking that our and other evidence suggests they have, what might this imply about their everyday thought and behavior? One possible implication is that, although they may see others as psychological beings who act, intend, perceive, feel, desire, know, and believe, they nevertheless do not see them as incessant "mental experiencers." That is, they do not envisage people as having a perpetually active inner life consisting of a steady stream of conscious ideation, or "roof-brain chatter," as someone called it (Farthing, 1992, p. 423). They represent them as creatures that see this, are afraid of that, want something else, and so on, but not as creatures that are experiencing, willy-nilly, a never-ending parade of mental contents, even when perceptually and behaviorally inactive.

Although the analogy would be misleading in other respects, in this respect their view of people is reminiscent of a common adult view of animals: namely, that animals tend to be mentally quiescent when perceptually and behaviorally quiescent and that they therefore have no rich and continuous inner life. This is not to say, of course, that adults never view other people in this subhuman way. Unfortunately, it happens all too commonly. Rather, it is to say that, unlike adults, young children may have no other option but to think of them this way, given the limitations on their knowledge of human consciousness. Because of these limitations, we would not expect young children to be trying to imagine the ongoing and recurrent inner concerns of their parents or other significant individuals in their lives: what these others might frequently be wishing or hoping for, worrying about, fantasizing about, and the like. Except when they have direct evidence for such concerns, they would never even be contemplated as possibilities.

This line of thinking suggests that our traditional view of children's perspective-taking development may not have been quite right: "For decades students of this development have been asking what mental content young children will attribute to others, for example, whether or not they will egocentrically misattribute their perspective to another person. Our data suggest that the question should sometimes be whether they are likely to attribute any mental content at all, egocentric or otherwise" (Flavell et al., 1993, pp. 396–397).

There are also possible implications for young children's thought and behavior regarding themselves as well as others. If, as we claim, they tend to be largely incognizant of their own ongoing mentation as well as that of others, one ought to see signs of it. For example, they should be less likely than older children and adults to know how they had arrived at a given decision, judgment, or problem solution because the mental steps leading up to it—its "mental history," so to speak—would be less accessible to them. They might also be less aware that they had become distracted from a previous task because they might not easily notice the change in the direction and content of their thinking. (They would also not easily realize that they were distracting others from whatever the others were thinking because they would be less likely to assume that the others *were* thinking.) Similarly, they should be less aware that they had changed their thinking about some topic because their previous ideas would be less available for comparison with their present ones. They should also show other deficits in cognitive monitoring, such as failures to notice their own uncertainty or their own incomprehension.

The research literature on metacognitive development shows that young children do exhibit such difficulties (e.g., Flavell, 1981; Markman, 1981). Indeed, to say, as developmental psychologists do, that young children are generally less given to metacognition than older ones is precisely to say that they are less given to reflect on their own mental events. Our findings concerning preschoolers' introspective limitations are thus quite consistent with a large body of evidence on their metacognitive limitations.

These findings are also consistent with clinical practice with children. A child psychiatrist friend assures us that child psychotherapists have generally found that children younger than about 8 or 9 are not suitable for the classical free-association, report-your-thoughts forms of therapy because they lack the necessary introspective abilities.

We would also expect that young children's introspective limitations would imply certain limitations in their conceptions of self. Farthing (1992, p. 13) has argued that the ability to think about one's own conscious experiences is necessary for an elaborated self-awareness, one that entails the realization that one is a unique individual, separate from others, with a unique personal history and future life course. The developmental literature also emphasizes the importance of self-reflection in developing a mature conception of one's self and one's personality (Damon & Hart, 1988; Harter, 1983). Much more so than young children's, older people's conceptions of self include representations of their continuous inner lives; they represent a subjective self as well as an objective self. Such conceptions are undoubtedly made possible by the acquisition of improved introspective skills: "Moreover, the adolescent is capable of introspection; one can reflect on one's own thoughts, feelings, and motives, which emerge as powerful new constructs in theorizing about the self and one's 'personality' " (Harter, 1983, p. 295).

DEVELOPMENTAL FACTORS

How do children increase their knowledge and awareness of thinking? It is of course possible that maturational factors play a developmental role, here as elsewhere. However, our ignorance of what such factors might be in this particular case makes it seem unprofitable to offer any speculations about them. It is easier to speculate about experiential factors that might help or hinder this development.

Let us examine possible hindrances to development first. As indicated in Chapter I, we now know that by the age of 4 or 5 years children have acquired some impressive basic knowledge about many aspects of the mental world. They seem to have achieved at least a fair understanding of what percepts, desires, emotions, intentions, knowledge, and beliefs are and how they relate to one another and to behavior. For example, they have learned that misleading perceptual input will cause a false belief and that the false belief will in turn cause maladaptive behavior that accords with that belief. As our and other studies show, children of this age have also learned some things about the mental activity of thinking of. However, they seem less knowledgeable about it than their understanding of these other mental entities might lead one to expect. Why might this be?

It may have to do with how salient and important thinking is to young children, relative to these other mental processes. Emotions are phenomenologically and behaviorally salient in the self and usually behaviorally salient in others. Similarly, there is often good evidence for what the self or another believes or desires, and the evidence may become even more noticeable when the belief proves false or the desire unsatisfiable. It is also often important for people to infer and communicate such mental states because it allows them to predict behavior and achieve desired goals. Consequently, young children and other people (parents, siblings, peers) are powerfully motivated to talk to one another about what they want, feel, believe, etc., and they often do so (e.g., Bartsch & Wellman, in press; Dunn, Brown, Slomkowski, Tesla, & Youngblade, 1991; Shatz, Wellman, & Silber, 1983).

All these things seem less true of the process of thinking or mental attention. Consider the case of an inactive person's idle stream of consciousness. If the person is another individual, there is liable to be no evidence for the stream's existence. If the person is the self, the stream may be quite nonsalient, especially qua mental process as distinguished from the external objects and events to which the mental process refers. The thinking may also have no immediate behavioral consequences that would strongly impel one to attend to it. As a consequence, people seldom find reason to talk to young children about the stream of consciousness, and there is no single word for it in everyday language for the people to use or the children to learn. Even the word *think,* which seems to be the best single term for unspecified mental activity, has its ambiguities: it is often used more narrowly to denote reasoning, problem solving, etc. and also often used to denote believing (thinking that vs. thinking of or about) or uncertainty (think vs. know). If the foregoing obstacles are real, it is not surprising that knowledge about thinking would be a relatively late development.

What experiences might facilitate this development? Perhaps certain kinds of thoughts become particularly noticeable to young children, especially when their attention is not otherwise engaged:

How might children come to discover the stream of consciousness? We obviously do not know but would venture the following speculation.

They may first become aware of it during the relatively brief and infrequent times in their day when they are awake but physically inactive, not actively engaged either perceptually or motorically with their world. Such a time for many children may be the period between going to bed and going to sleep. Some of the trains of thought that occur at such times might have two properties that would facilitate this awareness. On the one hand, they are charged with negative affect and are therefore impossible not to notice. An example might be the thought that there is or will be a monster in their darkened room, a common fear of young children. On the other hand, they may want to rid their minds of such thoughts but find they cannot; the thoughts stubbornly resist the children's efforts to suppress them. More generally, persistent worries and other preoccupations may be among the first examples of the stream of consciousness to be noticed by children. (Flavell et al., 1993, p. 396)

There is currently a controversy in the field as to how children acquire their knowledge about the mental world. Some argue that they acquire it largely through a process of naive theory construction (Gopnik & Wellman, 1992). Others argue that they acquire it primarily through a process of simulation or role taking, in which they imagine themselves in the other person's situation and assume that the person would be having the same mental states that they notice themselves having while taking the person's role (Harris, 1992).

We believe that both processes will prove to be important in explaining most developments in this area. Something like simulation may be particularly important in children's discovery of the stream of consciousness. That is, they may become increasingly aware of their own continuous mental experiences through the sorts of quiet-time observations just mentioned and then use this awareness to infer that other people are probably also having the same sorts of experiences, despite the absence of any observable evidence that they are. If other sources of evidence that conscious individuals experience a continuous flow of mental contents are as meager as we have suggested they might be, it is hard to see how children could come to this insight except by generalizing from their own experience of it. At the same time, something more akin to theory development could also be at least a minor contributor. As children become more and more aware of the many different sorts of mental states and activities that the mind can harbor, it may gradually dawn on them that it is a busier, more active place than they had previously imagined.

Finally, experiences associated with formal schooling may also promote knowledge and awareness of thinking. In formal school settings children are given cognitive tasks and problems and asked to do directed, sometimes effortful mental work in order to try to solve them. They may be asked to recall the mental steps leading up to their solution, to think again or think harder, to keep their minds on whatever they are supposed to be thinking or doing, or to do other things that call attention to mental activity. They also engage in verbal thinking in the form of reading, writing, and arithmetic calculations. Such verbal thinking is apt to be overt or semiovert in young learners and therefore relatively easy for them to detect and reflect on; they can literally hear themselves thinking. It has long been known that metacognition may facilitate school activities such as reading (e.g., Garner, 1987). The suggestion here is that the reverse may also be true: repeatedly engaging in such mental activities in school may facilitate children's knowledge and awareness of their own and other people's mental lives.

REFERENCES

Astington, J. W. (1993). *The child's discovery of the mind*. Cambridge, MA: Harvard University Press.

Baron-Cohen, S. (1991). The development of a theory of mind in autism: Deviance or delay? *Psychiatric Clinics of North America, 14,* 33–51.

Baron-Cohen, S., & Cross, P. (1992). Reading the eyes: Evidence for the role of perception in the development of a theory of mind. *Mind and Language, 7,* 172–186.

Bartsch, K., & Wellman, H. M. (in press). *Children talk about the mind*. New York: Oxford University Press.

Broughton, J. (1978). Development of concepts of self, mind, reality and knowledge. In W. Damon (Ed.), *Social cognition* (New Directions for Child Development, No. 1). San Francisco: Jossey-Bass.

Bruner, J. S. (1973). *Beyond the information given: Studies in the psychology of knowing*. New York: Norton.

Chandler, M. (1988). Doubt and developing theories of mind. In J. W. Astington, P. L. Harris, & D. R. Olson (Eds.), *Developing theories of mind*. New York: Cambridge University Press.

Cohen, J. (1993). *Children's understanding of spontaneous cognitive cueing*. Unpublished honor's thesis, Stanford University, Department of Psychology.

Damon, W., & Hart, D. (1988). *Self-understanding in childhood and adolescence*. New York: Cambridge University Press.

D'Andrade, R. (1987). A folk model of the mind. In D. Holland & N. Quinn (Eds.), *Cultural models in language and thought*. New York: Cambridge University Press.

Dolgin, K. G., & Behrend, D. A. (1984). Children's knowledge about animates and inanimates. *Child Development, 55,* 1646–1650.

Dunn, J., Brown, J., Slomkowski, C., Tesla, C., & Youngblade, L. (1991). Young children's understanding of other people's feelings and beliefs: Individual differences and their antecedents. *Child Development, 62,* 1352–1366.

Ericsson, K. A., & Simon, H. A. (1993). *Protocol analysis: Verbal reports as data* (2d ed.). Cambridge, MA: MIT Press.

Estes, D., & Buchanan, L. (1993, March). *Mental rotation and metacognition in early childhood*. Paper presented at the meeting of the Society for Research in Child Development, New Orleans.

Estes, D., Wellman, H. M., & Woolley, J. P. (1989). Children's understanding of mental phenomena. In H. Reese (Ed.), *Advances in child development and behavior* (Vol. **22**). New York: Academic.

Farthing, G. W. (1992). *The psychology of consciousness*. Englewood Cliffs, NJ: Prentice-Hall.

Flavell, J. H. (1981). Cognitive monitoring. In W. P. Dickson (Ed.), *Children's oral communication skills*. New York: Academic.

Flavell, J. H. (1993). Young children's understanding of thinking and consciousness. *Current Directions in Psychological Science, 2,* 40–43.

Flavell, J. H., Green, F. L., & Flavell, E. R. (1990). Developmental changes in children's knowledge about the mind. *Cognitive Development, 5,* 1–27.

Flavell, J. H., Green, F. L., & Flavell, E. R. (1993). Children's understanding of the stream of consciousness. *Child Development, 64,* 387–398.

Foley, M. A., & Johnson, M. K. (1985). Confusion between memories for performed and imagined actions. *Child Development, 56,* 1145–1155.

Garner, R. (1987). *Metacognition and reading comprehension*. Norwood, NJ: Ablex.

Gopnik, A., & Astington, J. (1988). Children's understanding of representational change and its relation to the understanding of false-belief and the appearance-reality distinction. *Child Development, 59,* 26–37.

Gopnik, A., & Graf, P. (1988). Knowing how you know: Young children's ability to identify and remember the sources of their beliefs. *Child Development, 59,* 1366–1371.

Gopnik, A., & Slaughter, V. (1991). Young children's understanding of changes in their mental states. *Child Development, 62,* 98–110.

Gopnik, A., & Wellman, H. M. (1992). Why the child's theory of mind really is a theory. *Mind and Language, 7,* 145–171.

Gordon, F. R., & Flavell, J. H. (1977). The development of intuitions about cognitive cueing. *Child Development, 48,* 1027–1033.

Hadwin, J., & Perner, J. (1991). Pleased and surprised: Children's cognitive theory of emotion. *British Journal of Developmental Psychology, 9,* 215–234.

Hansen, K. E. (1993). *Young children's understanding of the mediation of the mind in emotions: Emotional change as a result of cognitive cueing*. Unpublished honor's thesis, Stanford University, Department of Psychology.

Harris, P. L. (1992). From simulation to folk psychology: The case for development. *Mind and Language, 7,* 120–144.

Harter, S. (1983). Developmental perspectives on the self-system. In E. M. Hetherington (Ed.), P. H. Mussen (Series Ed.), *Handbook of child psychology: Vol. 4. Socialization, personality, and social development*. New York: Wiley.

James, W. (1890). *The principles of psychology* (Vol. 1). New York: Holt.

Johnson, C. N., & Wellman, H. M. (1982). Children's developing conceptions of the mind and brain. *Child Development, 53,* 222–234.

Johnson, M. K., Hashtroudi, S., & Lindsay, D. S. (1993). Source monitoring. *Psychological Bulletin, 114,* 3–28.

Laurendeau, M., & Pinard, A. (1962). *Causal thinking in the child*. New York: International Universities Press.

Leslie, A. M. (1988). Some implications for mechanisms underlying the child's theory of mind. In J. Astington, P. Harris, & D. Olson (Eds.), *Developing theories of mind*. New York: Cambridge University Press.

Lindsay, D. S., Johnson, M. K., & Kwon, P. (1991). Developmental changes in memory source monitoring. *Journal of Experimental Child Psychology, 52,* 297–318.

Lyon, T. D. (1993). *Young children's understanding of desire and knowledge*. Unpublished doctoral dissertation, Stanford University.

Markman, E. M. (1981). Comprehension monitoring. In W. P. Dickson (Ed.), *Children's oral communication skills*. New York: Academic.

Montgomery, D. E. (1992). Young children's theory of knowing: The development of a folk epistemology. *Developmental Review, 12,* 410–430.

Moses, L. J., & Chandler, M. J. (1992). Traveler's guide to children's theories of mind. *Psychological Inquiry,* **3,** 286–301.

Nisbett, R. E., & Wilson, T. D. (1977). Telling more than we can know: Verbal reports on mental processes. *Psychological Review,* **84,** 231–259.

O'Neill, D. K., Astington, J. W., & Flavell, J. H. (1992). Young children's understanding of the role that sensory experiences play in knowledge acquisition. *Child Development,* **63,** 474–490.

O'Neill, D. K., & Gopnik, A. (1991). Young children's ability to identify the sources of their beliefs. *Developmental Psychology,* **27,** 390–397.

Perner, J. (1991). *Understanding the representational mind.* Cambridge, MA: MIT Press.

Piaget, J. (1929). *The child's conception of the world.* London: Routledge & Kegan Paul.

Piaget, J. (1976). *The grasp of consciousness: Action and concept in the young child.* Cambridge, MA: Harvard University Press.

Pillow, B. H. (1988). Young children's understanding of attentional limits. *Child Development,* **59,** 38–46.

Pillow, B. H. (1989a). The development of beliefs about selective attention. *Merrill-Palmer Quarterly,* **35,** 421–443.

Pillow, B. H. (1989b). Early understanding of perception as a source of knowledge. *Journal of Experimental Child Psychology,* **47,** 116–129.

Pillow, B. H. (in press). Two trends in the development of conceptual perspective-taking: An elaboration of the passive-active hypothesis. *International Journal of Behavioral Development.*

Pope, K. S., & Singer, J. L. (1978). Some dimensions of the stream of consciousness: Towards a model of ongoing thought. In G. E. Schwartz & D. Shapiro (Eds.), *Consciousness and self-regulation: Advances in research* (Vol. **2**). New York: Holt.

Pratt, C., & Bryant, P. (1990). Young children understand that looking leads to knowing (so long as they are looking into a single barrel). *Child Development,* **61,** 973–982.

Ramsey, W. (1993). *The philosophy and psychology of folk psychology.* Unpublished manuscript, University of Notre Dame.

Rosenkrantz, S. L. (1991). *Children's recognition of the facial expressions associated with cognitive states.* Unpublished manuscript, Stanford University, Department of Psychology.

Schneider, W., & Sodian, B. (1988). Metamemory-memory behavior relationships in young children: Evidence from a memory-for-location task. *Journal of Experimental Child Psychology,* **45,** 209–233.

Schwanenflugel, P. J., Fabricius, W. V., & Alexander, J. (in press). Developing theories of mind: Understanding concepts and relations between mental activities. *Child Development.*

Shatz, M., Wellman, H. M., & Silber, S. (1983). The acquisition of mental verbs: A systematic investigation of first references to mental state. *Cognition,* **14,** 301–321.

Sodian, B., & Schneider, W. (1990). Children's understanding of cognitive cuing: How to manipulate cues to fool a competitor. *Child Development,* **61,** 697–704.

Taylor, M. (1988). The development of the seeing-knowing distinction. In J. W. Astington, P. L. Harris, & D. R. Olson (Eds.), *Developing theories of mind.* New York: Cambridge University Press.

Wegner, D. M., Schneider, D. J., Carter, S. R., & White, T. L. (1987). Paradoxical effects of thought suppression. *Journal of Personality and Social Psychology,* **53,** 5–13.

Wellman, H. M. (1990). *The child's theory of mind.* Cambridge, MA: MIT Press.

Wellman, H. M., & Estes, D. (1986). Early understanding of mental entities: A reexamination of childhood realism. *Child Development,* **57,** 910–923.

Wellman, H. M., & Gelman, S. A. (1992). Cognitive development: Foundational theories of core domains. *Annual Review of Psychology,* **43,** 337–375.

Wimmer, H., Hogrefe, J., & Sodian, B. (1988). A second stage in children's conception of mental life: Understanding informational accesses as origins of knowledge and belief. In J. W. Astington, P. L. Harris, & D. R. Olson (Eds.), *Developing theories of mind.* New York: Cambridge University Press.

Woolley, J. D., & Wellman, H. M. (1992). Children's conceptions of dreams. *Cognitive Development,* **7,** 365–380.

Woolley, J. D., & Wellman, H. M. (1993). Origin and truth: Young children's understanding of the relation of imaginary mental representations. *Child Development,* **64,** 1–17.

Yuill, N. (1984). Young children's coordination of motive and outcome in judgments of satisfaction and morality. *British Journal of Developmental Psychology,* **2,** 73–81.

ACKNOWLEDGMENTS

This research was supported by National Institute of Mental Health grant MH 40687. We are grateful to the children, teachers, and parents of Stanford University's Bing School, Arboretum Preschool, and Community Child Center; the Peninsula School in Menlo Park; the Keys School in Palo Alto; the Palo Alto Jewish Community Center Summer Camp; and the Foothill College Summer Youth Camp. Their cooperation made these studies possible. We are also indebted to Fred Dretske, Alison Gopnik, Guven Guzeldere, Paul Harris, Marcia Johnson, Angeline Lillard, Tom Lyon, Ellen Markman, Daniela O'Neill, Kyrie Robinson, Roger Shepard, Laura Townsend, and other colleagues and students for their helpful suggestions over the course of this project. Please direct correspondence to John H. Flavell, Department of Psychology, Stanford University, Stanford, CA 94305.

Paul L. Harris

John Flavell and his colleagues provide a two-pronged demonstration: young preschool children are surprisingly mentalistic in their conception of thinking; at the same time, they are surprisingly ill attuned to the ongoing process of thinking. They show little appreciation of the incessant and sequential nature of the stream of consciousness. In a masterly final chapter, this latter insensitivity is explained in terms of young children's ignorance of the causal connections among successive thoughts: they appear to conceive of thinking as an intermittent process that occasionally alights on a given referent, in a relatively unconstrained and unpredictable fashion.

In the comments that follow, I want to stress some of the positive aspects of preschoolers' conception of thinking—aspects that we might not have given credence to until quite recently but that fit nicely into an increasingly well-established picture. Second, I would like to raise some questions about the relatively negative portrait that is drawn of the young child's introspective abilities. I seek to do this in two ways. First, I ask whether there really is no evidence of introspection among young preschoolers. Second, I underline the special, and potentially restrictive, definition of that capacity that is adopted in this *Monograph*.

The Preschooler as Mentalist

The findings from Chapter II, particularly those from Studies 1–3 in which 3-year-olds were included, provide a persuasive demonstration that the preschool child is a mentalist, in the sense that he or she does not confuse thinking with other activities such as seeing, talking, or touching. Thus, children realize at this age that someone may be doing nothing overtly but may at the same time be thinking. In addition, they realize that thinking is an intentional activity that is directed at a target that may or may not be currently present (Study 2). As Flavell and his colleagues put it, this evidence shows that "preschoolers have at least a minimal grasp of the bare-bones essentials of thinking: namely, that it is some sort of internal, mental activity that people engage in that refers to real or imaginary objects or events" (p. 78).

This mentalistic stance has recently surfaced in parallel work on children's concept of emotions. The spontaneous conversation of 3- and even 2-year-old children shows that they think of emotions such as fear, anger, and happiness as mental states that can lead to overt action and external indices but that are not equivalent to those actions and indices. In addition, they grasp the intentionality of such states: they talk cogently of the entities that people are afraid of, mad at, or happy about (Wellman, Harris, Banerjee, & Sinclair, in press).

The experimental findings of this *Monograph*, and of discourse-based research on children's mental state concepts by Wellman and his colleagues (Bartsch & Wellman, in press; Wellman et al., in press), amount to a convincing demonstration, in my view, that young children, including 3-year-olds, share certain key assumptions about the mind with adults. I stress this point because considerable effort has been invested in showing that the preschool child, notably the 3-year-old, does not share one central assumption about the mind with adults. Thus, it has been argued that 3-year-olds lack the allegedly key notion of the mind as a representational device (Perner, 1991). These claims are not incompatible with one another, but we must not allow preoccupation with the latter to obscure the importance of the former.

Introspection by Preschool Children?

Chapter IV leads to the conclusion that young children are quite poor at introspection. For example, when 5-year-olds were asked to sit in a chair and think about where they kept their toothbrush, the majority were unable to recall a few seconds later what they had been thinking about when seated in the chair (Studies 11 and 12). Even when explicitly asked if they had been thinking about their bathroom, a substantial proportion denied that they had done so. In Chapter IV, only children aged 5 years and older were tested, but it seems plausible to conclude that 3- and 4-year-olds would have fared even more poorly. Should we conclude then that preschool children are poor at introspection, and can we square that conclusion with the assertion made above that they have a mentalistic conception of thinking?

In a provocative study, Estes, Wellman, and Woolley (1989) asked children to form a mental image ("make a picture in your head") of a familiar object such as a pair of scissors. Children were then asked whether they could transform this mental image through thought alone. For example, children were asked, "Just by thinking real hard, without moving your hands, can you make them [i.e., the scissors] open and close?" Five-year-olds mostly agreed that they could carry out this mental transformation. By contrast, 3- and 4-year-olds responded unsystematically. About half the children in each age group said that they could make the transformation, half that they could not. These skeptical children were asked to try in any case and then questioned again about whether they had succeeded. At this point, almost all the 3- and 4-year-olds said that they had succeeded. A control procedure showed that this change of opinion was not just the result of repeated probing. When taken through a similar procedure with respect to an actual pair of scissors (placed in a box), most 3- and 4-year-olds immediately insisted that they could not make them open and close just by thinking, and they reiterated this conclusion after being asked to try to do so (Estes et al., 1989, p. 61, fig. 3).

These data suggest two important points: that 3- and 4-year-olds can provide introspective reports on their own thought processes and that they can learn something about those thought processes (namely, that it is possible to imagine an object in motion) from introspection. As Estes et al. (1989) conclude, such findings "provide evidence against the claim that there is little basis in untutored experience to inspire introspective reports and that the ability to provide such reports must be slowly acquired through socialization" (p. 84).

The findings and conclusion of Estes et al. (1989) are not easy to reconcile with those of Flavell and his colleagues. In the penultimate paragraph of their *Monograph*, they do attest to the potentially instructive role of introspection and underline the limitations of naive theory construction. Still, their findings mostly suggest that 3-year-olds are poor at introspection and unlikely to profit from it.

How can this discrepancy be explained? There are at least three possibilities: one concerns the way in which the dialogue between experimenter and child is conducted, one the nature of the introspected process, and one the possibility that there are different levels of introspection. I begin with this last possibility.

Levels of Introspection

Flavell and his colleagues argue that it is important to distinguish between two different cases. On the one hand, children might report what they have, in fact, been thinking about (e.g., the crayons that children were asked to compare in Studies 11 and 12) but construe their report "as a factual report of the external objects or events encountered . . . rather than as an introspective, reflective consciousness–type report of thoughts concerning them." On the other hand, children can construe what they are doing as "reporting mental activity concerning the task objects and events rather than as just reporting the presence of the objects and events themselves" (p. 75). Flavell and his colleagues emphasize that it is only the latter type of report that amounts to genuine introspection.

Can we dismiss the reports of the 3- and 4-year-olds tested by Estes et al. (1989) as not being genuinely introspective? More specifically, did the children think that they were reporting on the objects that they were thinking about rather than their mental activity? This is obviously most unlikely. Children explicitly recognized that such transformations could not be applied to a real pair of scissors, only to the pair of scissors that they were visualizing. By this definition, then, we do appear to be dealing with genuine introspection.

The Nature of the Introspected Process

It seems reasonable to suppose that certain mental processes are easier to introspect about than others. In particular, it is possible that visual imagery—of the type prompted by Estes et al. (1989)—is more readily open to genuine introspection than some of the decision processes or cases of puzzlement that Flavell and his colleagues prompted. First, because imagery is often concerned with nonexistent objects or events, there may be less temptation to construe a report as merely describing an external situation. Second, leaving cases of pathology aside, we readily assume that our visual images have an internal, mental source rather than an external source. By contrast, for many other mental products—for example, the apparently discrete sequence of words that we hear when someone speaks to us—it is tempting to assume a purely external origin even though spectrographic analysis shows quite convincingly that we must be imposing a mental discontinuity on a physically continuous input. These two considerations tie in with several observations made by Flavell and his colleagues. Preschool children are inclined to think of mental activity as something that does not engage the external world. It is not necessary for looking at a picture or understanding a story.

In sum, then, there are grounds for thinking that children's capacity for genuine introspection might vary with the type of cognitive process under consideration. Until this possibility is more thoroughly explored, we should be cautious in assuming that 3-year-olds are consistently poor at introspection.

The Dialogue between Child and Experimenter

In assessing children's capacity for introspection, Flavell and his colleagues engaged children in a dialogue with the experimenter, and they defined *genuine* introspection as the capacity to provide a report (construed as a report of mental activity) while so engaged. This is a pragmatic approach, but it is not without risk. The risk is that developments in the capacity for dialogue-based recall may be misconstrued as developments in the capacity for introspection itself.

I can convey this worry by means of an analogy. Research on children's memory is currently flourishing. A common procedure in this research is to engage young children in a dialogue about some past event. This seems a reasonable tactic because a great deal of children's memory activity about the past is likely to be prompted, and indeed nurtured, by dialogue with adults (Nelson, 1993). However, any deficiencies that children show during such a dialogue can have two different explanations. First, they may have forgotten the episode in question. Alternatively, they may remember the episode but not be cued to retrieve it by the particular conversational prompts provided by the adult. Ploys such as "Tell me about the last time that we went to the zoo" may be a less effective reminder than some other cue such as the badge or picture book bought during that last visit. In sum, children's ability to engage in a dialogue about the past is certainly worthy of study in its own right, but it may not reveal all that children can remember about the past. The same consideration applies to studies of introspection: children's ability to engage in a dialogue about their past thoughts or immediately preceding thoughts is worth studying, but it may not reveal all that children notice and remember about their thoughts.

Flavell and his colleagues offer a very persuasive interpretation of the limited introspection evinced by younger children. They argue that younger children tend to construe thoughts as isolated and disconnected rather than as continuous and connected. This conception of thinking places them at a disadvantage when they are invited to recall their thoughts. They do not recognize that past events are likely to have triggered certain thoughts. As a result, they are hampered in reactivating any memory of the thoughts that they had.

I think that this account is both fascinating and plausible. Yet it also carries a sting in its tail, one that remained relatively unexplored in the sequence of 14 studies. The sting is that 3-year-olds might just prove quite good at introspection if one could bypass the limitations that they show in dialogue-based retrieval, just as very young children's memory for past episodes may prove quite accurate if one can bypass some of their limitations in ordinary conversation about the past.

Suppose that the adult engages the child in a conversation about some ongoing or just completed mental activity and refers to that activity in ways that the child can readily understand, for example, by referring explicitly to some mental content that the child has been contemplating. Under these circumstances, retrieval problems should be lessened, and the child ought to be capable of reporting on the activity in question. This is, of course, the type of procedure that Estes et al. (1989) used. Consistent with this observation, 5-year-olds were more accurate at recognition than recall in both Study 11 and Study 12.

Conclusions

Having raised some questions about whether preschool children are consistently limited in their introspective capacity, I want to underline the plausibility of the main claim that is advanced in this *Monograph:* that there is a sharp improvement during the preschool and early school years in children's introspective abilities. That rise is explained in a cogent and satisfying way by the proposal that young children are gradually acquiring an understanding of the causal connectedness of the stream of consciousness. My hunch is that this bold and persuasive hypothesis will give rise to a plethora of new research on children's self-reflective monitoring.

Consider just one theme that is briefly mentioned by Flavell and his colleagues. As adults we are aware of the way in which strong emotion floods our consciousness; we engage in intense rumination about events that have triggered our emotions, and such rumination often has an involuntary intensity that temporarily displaces thoughts of more routine or mundane matters. We might say that the causal connections among successive thoughts become tighter and narrower, as compared to the looser, less restrictive connections that link our meandering thoughts in moments of relaxation. In the case of traumatic events, such tight connections have a recurrent character in the form of repeated flashbacks.

To what extent are young children aware of this variation in the flow of consciousness? Are they especially likely to report on those emotionally charged thoughts that are involuntary or difficult to suppress? When do they begin to take steps to redirect or suppress such thoughts? There is some evidence that 8-year-olds appreciate how the flow of consciousness can be managed following a distressing event such as separation from parents (Harris, 1989): they try to keep busy and to avoid reminders of home. For the most part, however, young children's understanding of the relation between emotion, memory, and consciousness has not been explored. The *Monograph* by John Flavell and his colleagues shows us how to get started on that exciting research program.

References

Bartsch, K., & Wellman, H. M. (in press). *Children talk about the mind.* New York: Oxford University Press.

Estes, D., Wellman, H. M., & Woolley, J. D. (1989). Children's understanding of mental phenomena. In H. W. Reese (Ed.), *Advances in child development and behavior.* San Diego: Academic.

Harris, P. L. (1989). *Children and emotion.* Oxford: Blackwell.

Nelson, K. (1993). The psychological and social origins of autobiographical memory. *Psychological Science,* **4,** 7–14.

Perner, J. (1991). *Understanding the representational mind.* Cambridge, MA: Bradford, MIT Press.

Wellman, H. M., Harris, P. L., Banerjee, M., & Sinclair, A. (in press). Early understandings of emotion: Evidence from natural language. *Cognition and Emotion.*

COMMENTARY

TALKING IT OVER WITH MY BRAIN

Janet Wilde Astington

Given the abundance of research in the past decade revealing preschool children's understanding of the mind, you might think that there is nothing left for the researcher to investigate and little left for the 5-year-old to discover. You would be wrong on both counts, as Flavell, Green, and Flavell's *Monograph* neatly demonstrates. Almost all that has been written in the last 10 years has focused on children's knowledge of mental states rather than their knowledge of mental activity, which is the focus of the present work. This *Monograph* is thus most welcome, dealing as it does with a neglected aspect of this currently lively area of research. Moreover, it uncovers some surprising gaps in the preschooler's much-publicized theory of mind. The authors investigate three different aspects of children's knowledge about thinking: their ability to differentiate thinking from other activities, their awareness that thinking is always going on in people's minds, and their ability to introspect about their own thinking. Important developments in understanding the second and particularly the third of these aspects do not come until the early school years. Indeed, I will argue that schooling itself may have much to do with these developments. However, to begin with, I will consider the authors' findings in more detail.

The first set of studies, dealing with children's ability to differentiate thinking from other activities (Chap. II), connects with and elaborates earlier work in the field. Observational and experimental investigations of children's production and comprehension of mental terms have been going on since the early 1970s. We know that children use the term *think* from the age of 2 years or so (Bretherton & Beeghly, 1982; Limber, 1973). The first uses may be primarily to express uncertainty ("I think . . .") or to suggest an activity ("I thought we'd . . ."). However, 3-year-olds appropriately use the term to refer to mental states, sometimes to express the idea that what they think is different from what somebody else thinks or different from what they themselves thought earlier ("The people thought Dracula was mean but he was nice"; Shatz, Wellman, & Silber, 1983, p. 309). Earlier work also revealed that 4-year-olds appropriately distinguish the term *think* from such related mental terms as *know* and *remember*. For example, Johnson and Maratsos (1977) showed that 4-year-olds do not treat thinking as equivalent to saying and they understand that, although knowing presumes truth, thinking can be false. Similarly, 4-year-olds recognize that someone who says "I know p" or "I remember p" presupposes that the proposition p is true but someone who says "I think p" implies uncertainty concerning the truth of p (Abbeduto & Rosenberg, 1985; Moore, Bryant, & Furrow, 1989).

The studies reported in Chapter II likewise show that 3- and 4-year-olds have a well-developed understanding of the term *think*. They can distinguish thinking about an object from looking at it or acting on it or talking about it. They understand that one does not need to be able to see or to hear in order to think and that one can think about absent things. I have some worry that Study 1 may just train children to interpret "think bubbles," but it is interesting that they learn so easily, and, anyway, this concern applies only to the first study. Later studies in Chapter II show that 4- and 5-year-olds can distinguish between thinking and knowing, in situations where a person may be thinking or not thinking about an object when she does or does not know where it is. However, it may be that the children treat the situations as typical problem-solving cases—if you do not know where something is, you try to find it, that is, you think about it. In Study 4, they really succeed only in the condition where someone *is thinking* about an object and *does not know* its location.

This interpretation is supported by the results of Study 5, in which the experimenters reduced the processing load, telling the children whether the person was or was not thinking about x and then asking if she knew where x was. Thus, when told that she was thinking about x, they said that she does not know where it is. However, in this task, some of the children were also able to associate not thinking about x with either knowing or not knowing its location, depending on other conditions, and Study 6 extends these findings to situations other than those involving lost objects. Here, the experimenter suggested something that another adult was not currently thinking about, and then the experimenter asked the child whether the adult knew about that thing. But what if the adult started to think about the thing once it had been mentioned? We do not know whether this would occur to the children, but, if it did, then thinking and knowing would not be dissociated in the way the authors claim. I suppose that they could have asked the children whether the adult knew it at the beginning, when she was not thinking about it, but this is a very small point. More important, the study seems to tell us more about 4-year-olds' understanding of knowing than about their understanding of thinking as a mental activity.

Taken together, the studies in Chapter II certainly show that 3- and 4-year-olds understand that thinking is not the same as looking, talking, doing, or knowing. However, *thinking* in these studies is not so much the "ongoing mental activity" of the authors' introduction as "problem solving," usually with some behavioral association, such as losing something, or the adoption of a stereotypical facial expression or pose. A major problem is that, considered simply as ongoing mental activity, *thinking* does not have any behavioral indices. It is therefore difficult for children to acquire knowledge about it and for researchers to investigate children's knowledge about it. For example, in the first study, "The experimenter began by modeling thinking for the subjects. She gave the topic of what she would think about, namely, her bedroom, and then described some of its contents. The subject was encouraged to do the same" (p. 7). This captures the idea of *thinking* as "paying attention to something," but thinking about something is not the same as talking about it.

The second set of studies investigates children's awareness that thinking, or something like it, is always going on in a person's mind (Chap. III). In some of their earlier work, the authors showed that 4-year-olds do not assume that some sort of mental activity ("stream of consciousness") goes on continuously while a person is awake (Flavell, Green, & Flavell, 1993). The studies in Chapter III continue this investigation and show that the earlier work did not underestimate 4-year-olds' understanding. *Thinking* seems not to be the right term here, and the experimenters do not use it in the tasks. They asked, "Do you think anything is going on in her mind, or *not?*" (Study 7, p. 29), or, "Is her mind . . . *doing* something, or is her mind . . . *not doing* anything?" (supported by pretraining on a forced choice between two cartoon drawings) (Study 8, p. 36). In one task, they also gave children a very clear forced choice between two people's opinions: either "It doesn't *look like* anything is going on in her mind, so probably nothing is going on," or "Something is always going on in people's minds, so there *must* be something going on" (Study 8, p. 36).

The remarkable finding from these studies is that 4-year-olds generally do not attribute mental activity to another person, even one who is looking at or listening to a stimulus. In the easier task they do attribute mental activity to a person who is solving a problem (consistent with the results in Chap. II), but in the harder task they do not attribute mental activity to a person who is talking, reading, or deciding, and even 5-year-olds do not attribute mental activity to a person who is looking at a picture or listening to a story.

These results are reassuringly similar to those obtained by Johnson and Wellman (1982) more than 10 years ago, as the authors point out. Johnson and Wellman asked children, "Do you need your brain to do *x?*" where *x* was one of 30 different possibilities, such as dream, feel sad, tell a story, kick a ball, cough, smell something, and so on. They found that 4- and 5-year-olds think that the brain is necessary for cognitive tasks, such as thinking and remembering, but deny that it is needed for more perceptual tasks, such as looking or hearing, or motor tasks, such as walking.

Indeed, in the case of perceptual and motor tasks, there is no good reason why, without more knowledge of physiology, one should assume either that "you need your brain" (in Johnson and Wellman's terms) or that there is "something going on in his mind" (the phrase that Flavell et al. use). In ordinary language, children are told to "use your eyes" when they fail to see something in a picture, for example. As the authors suggest, young children may think that the eyes function in some way independently of the brain and are all that is needed for seeing and looking. Similarly, they may think that the ears are all that is needed for hearing and listening. Seeing and hearing are more passive than looking and listening. Possibly, there might be an intermediate stage at which children believe that the eyes are sufficient for seeing but that the brain is also required for looking or that the ears are sufficient for hearing but that the brain is also required for listening.

The last two studies in Chapter III further investigate 3–5-year-olds' ability to infer from a situation and from a person's behavior that she is thinking and what she is and is not thinking about. Even here, although the children can again infer that a person is thinking from her expression and pose, before 5 years they are not very good at inferring what the person is thinking about. The general impression is that, although preschoolers understand some aspects of thinking, there is still a lot that they do not know. They recognize thinking as a sort of mental process associated with problem solving. They have less understanding of it as constant, ongoing mental activity. Why do they not have this understanding? Do they have no awareness of their own stream of consciousness? Here we come to the most interesting and puzzling of the current findings.

The studies reported in Chapter IV investigate 5–8-year-olds' ability to introspect, that is, to examine their own thoughts. In general, 5-year-olds are not good at reporting either *that* they have been thinking or *what* they have been thinking about—despite some good efforts on the part of the experimenters to make *thinking about* very clear to the children. The authors suggest that the preschool children in Gopnik and Slaughter's (1991) study, who appear to be able to introspect, might not have been remembering what they had thought but what they had said. In Gopnik and Slaughter's study, 3- and 4-year-olds first entertained one mental state, such as a belief that there were crayons inside a crayon box. Then the state was changed (i.e., they discovered that there was something else in the box), and they were asked what they had thought was in the box before it was opened. The 4-year-olds could report their earlier belief, but the 3-year-olds could not, although they could report some of their earlier mental states that were later changed, such as pretenses and perceptions.

In their Study 12, where 5-year-olds' performance is somewhat improved, Flavell et al. caution us that the children may have been talking about the *content* of their thoughts, not about the *process* of thinking. The same explanation would apply to Gopnik and Slaughter's tasks, when children were questioned about the content of earlier beliefs, pretenses, desires, and so on—what they reported was the content of those mental states. That is, we do not need to think that the children were merely remembering what they had said. Indeed, in an earlier study (Gopnik & Astington, 1988), children were not asked to *say*, for example, what they thought was in the box before opening it; even so, the 4- and 5-year-olds were able to report their earlier beliefs. We can accept this and still accept the current finding that 5-year-olds are not very good at reporting that they have been thinking—the activity, not the content. That is to say, young children may be able to introspect about the content of their mental states without recognizing them as produced by their mind's activity.

For Flavell et al. introspection is reflecting and reporting on "mental events *construed as mental events by the reflecting person*" (p. 74; my emphasis). That is, introspection consists of a report, not just of the thought content, but of the thinking process. Thus, in Gopnik's tasks, when children report, for example, that they thought that there were crayons in the crayon box, this is not an instance of introspection in Flavell et al.'s terms. But then again it might be—because, as they point out, in many cases we cannot distinguish between a report of the content and a report of the process. Mental states (i.e., intentional mental states) consist of a propositional attitude toward a propositional content. At first, children may be more aware of contents than attitudes. It may be—indeed, it almost certainly is—the case that we talk more about contents than about attitudes. Is this why preschoolers have such a good understanding of mental states, as all the theory-of-mind research of the last ten years shows, and such poor knowledge of mental activity, as the current work so clearly demonstrates?

As the authors point out, "people seldom find reason to talk to young children about the stream of consciousness, and there is no single word for it in everyday language for the people to use or the children to learn" (p. 89; see also Flavell et al., 1993). This is certainly true and may be a large part of the reason why preschoolers do so poorly in the tasks reported here. In an extensive study of preschoolers' natural language use of mental terms, Bartsch and Wellman (in press) coded children's use of *think* as belief, as imagination, and as mental activity. They give many examples of the first two uses, but only one of the third: "Adam at 2;11 said: 'I . . . just thinking.'

Adult: 'You're just thinking?' Adam: 'Yes.' Adult: 'What are you thinking about?' Adam: 'Thinking 'bout leaf' " (Bartsch & Wellman, in press). Interestingly, even in this example, the adult turns the conversation in the direction of the thought content.

In ordinary language use, we might compare the terms *think* and *breathe*. Both thinking and breathing are going on all the time, but unnoticed and not talked about—except in marked cases, such as when the doctor says, "Breathe in," and the child does so in an exaggerated way or when the child has lost a toy and the parent says, "Think where you were last playing with it." When we adults are sitting quietly and someone asks, "Are you thinking?" we might say, "No," if we are not currently pondering or deciding something, even though we are aware of the stream of consciousness. So how do children learn about this? How do they come to know that they are breathing or thinking? They learn that they are, not from experience, or at least not just from experience, but from having the experience brought to their attention and labeled for them. Harris (1989) asserts that even very young children are well aware of their own mental states, but wonders how they come to think of them in terms of beliefs and desires, and then speculates, "Does the community offer the child a way of talking, a gloss, that provides instruction in how to conceptualize mental states? . . . Is there some hitherto uncharted conjunction between the innate structure of experience and linguistic instruction?" (Harris, 1989, p. 80). I think that there is; I think that language is fundamental to children's conceptualization of the mental world.

This means that any attempt to assess young children's understanding has to be supremely sensitive to the way the children themselves might talk about these things. Flavell et al. are well aware of this problem and asked the children not only whether they were "thinking" or "wondering" but whether their "mind was shining on anything" (after a demonstration of how a flashlight shines, illuminating some things and not others). The analogy seemed to be clear enough to the 8-year-olds but did not appear to help the 5-year olds. One wonders what phrase would come naturally to young children. How would they themselves talk about it? At the beginning of Study 8, the experimenters asked the 4-year-old subjects the open question, "Do you know what your brain or mind does?" (p. 35). Only seven of the 24 children questioned offered any answer, and most of those replied, "Thinks," but one said, "Sometimes it talks to me" (p. 38). This may seem a bizarre response, but it may be the way children first experience self-reflection—as a dialogue with their brain! The idea is conveyed in a rhyme that used to be broadcast on the television program "Sesame Street":

I have a mind and my mind helps me, in everything I do and see. *My mind tells me,* here is a ball. . . .

Recently, Bruce Homer and I have been investigating children's ability to reflect on their own false beliefs, analogous to their ability to understand others' second-order beliefs (Perner & Wimmer, 1985). That is, we are interested in whether children realize that, when they held a false belief, they did not really know the truth even though they thought they did. The children were shown something that was not what it appeared to be, and then they discovered their mistake, as in Gopnik and Astington's (1988) study. For example, in one task, a crayon box contained a little doll; in another, what appeared to be a cat's ears when only part of a picture could be seen turned out to be the petals of a flower. Once the materials had been returned to their original state, the children were first asked whether they had known what it was at the beginning and then whether they had thought that they knew. In two protocols, 5-year-olds refer to what their mind or brain told them:

> Experimenter: Did you know what the picture was before we turned the page?
> Subject 1: No.
> E: Did you think you knew?
> S1: I said it . . . what my mind told me.
> E: What?
> S1: I thought I knew.

> Experimenter: Did you know what was inside the box before we opened it?
> Subject 2: No.
> E: Did you think you knew?
> S2: My brain was telling me it was crayons, but really I knew it was a doll.

It may be that children's first experiences of introspection are perceived, not as reflection on their own thoughts, but as listening to what their brain has to say! There is other evidence that 5-year-olds may sometimes regard their brain as a sort of alter ego. A colleague reports that, on finding that her mother would not allow her to escape responsibility for an action by claiming that she had not done it on purpose, her 5-year-old daughter claimed that her brain had done it, not she herself. I wonder whether we might help young children introspect about their thoughts by asking them what their brain (or mind) is telling them. We could give a Vygotskian explanation to such a possibility. Children first reflect on their thoughts in conversation with an adult, then in self-reflection, but there is an intermediate stage during which they experience self-reflection as the voice of their brain. Perhaps this is enhanced when they hear themselves talking aloud to themselves—children's egocentric, private, or self-directed speech (Berk, 1992).

In the same vein, Flavell, Green, and Flavell suggest that participation in formal school activities may facilitate children's introspective abilities. They say that children's thinking about school tasks may be overt and therefore easy for them to reflect on: "They can literally hear themselves thinking" (p. 91). Certainly, children do talk to themselves about tasks in the classroom. Moreover, competent children do this more than less competent ones, perhaps because not all their cognitive capacity is occupied by the immediate demands of the task, as Meichenbaum and Biemiller (1992) suggest. It may well be that such self-directed talk fosters children's awareness of their own thought processes and develops their ability to introspect.

Indeed, Vygotsky argued that "school instruction . . . plays a decisive role in making the child conscious of his own mental activities" (1931/1962, p. 92). What other aspects of schooling might be of importance? Perhaps it is teachers' talk about mental activity, as Flavell et al. suggest, although we do not know how much of this actually goes on in school classrooms (Olson & Astington, 1993). Perhaps it is the acquisition of literate skills, again suggested by Flavell et al. Donaldson (1978) has argued that, when children learn to read, they gain a reflective awareness of language that may lead them to reflective awareness of thought itself: "Thus it turns out that those very features of the written word which encourage awareness of language may also encourage awareness of one's own thinking and be relevant to the development of intellectual self-control" (Donaldson, 1978, p. 95).

Olson (1994) explores in detail the ways in which literacy leads to the development of subjectivity, which he relates to self-consciousness and which he defines as "recognition of one's own and others' mental states as mental states" (p. 234). He traces this development both in the individual child and in terms of cultural history. This suggests another important issue. Is the conception of a stream of consciousness a universal notion, or is it peculiar to a literate theory of mind? Is the ability to introspect essentially a product of Western schooling?

In the abundance of research on children's developing theories of mind that has been published in the last decade, there are very few studies that investigate this development in unschooled, nonliterate populations. There may be a universal tendency to explain and predict human action by consideration of beliefs and desires (Avis & Harris, 1991), but it does not necessarily follow that what we call *belief* and *desire* are conceptualized in the same way in all cultures. These states may be thought of as internal and private, or they may have a more external quality. The Quechua, for example, refer to what something looks like rather than what somebody might think that it is (McCormick, 1994). The Greeks of Homer's time thought that people's activities were due more to the will of the gods than to individuals' own desires (Snell, 1948/1982). Indeed, they experienced their thoughts as the voices of the gods. Perhaps the 5-year-old who referred to what his brain told him was interpreting the same phenomenon in terms of our culture's way of talking.

The voice of the gods, the voice of the brain, private speech—are these but different ways of conceptualizing introspection? Flavell (1992) writes of how his early work on private speech led to his interest in metamemory, which led to his interest in metacognition more generally considered, which later became part of the field of children's theory of mind. Perhaps I might suggest that his most recent work in this field, in the area of introspection, turns his research program full circle back to children's private speech.

References

Abbeduto, L., & Rosenberg, S. (1985). Children's knowledge of the presuppositions of know and other cognitive verbs. *Journal of Child Language*, **12**, 621–641.

Avis, J., & Harris, P. L. (1991). Belief-desire reasoning among Baka children: Evidence for a universal conception of mind. *Child Development*, **62**, 460–467.

Bartsch, K., & Wellman, H. M. (in press). *Children talk about the mind.* New York: Oxford University Press.

Berk, L. E. (1992). Children's private speech: An overview of theory and the status of research. In R. M. Diaz & L. E. Berk (Eds.), *Private speech: From social interaction to self-regulation.* Hillsdale, NJ: Erlbaum.

Bretherton, I., & Beeghly, M. (1982). Talking about internal states: The acquisition of an explicit theory of mind. *Developmental Psychology*, **18**, 906–921.

Donaldson, M. (1978). *Children's minds.* Glasgow: Fontana.

Flavell, J. H. (1992). Perspectives on perspective taking. In H. Beilin & P. Pufall (Eds.), *Piaget's theory: Prospects and possibilities.* Hillsdale, NJ: Erlbaum.

Flavell, J. H., Green, F. L., & Flavell, E. R. (1993). Children's understanding of the stream of consciousness. *Child Development*, **64**, 387–398.

Gopnik, A., & Astington, J. W. (1988). Children's understanding of representational change and its relation to the understanding of false belief and the appearance-reality distinction. *Child Development*, **59**, 26–37.

Gopnik, A., & Slaughter, V. (1991). Young children's understanding of changes in their mental states. *Child Development*, **62**, 98–110.

Harris, P. L. (1989). *Children and emotion.* Oxford: Blackwell.

Johnson, C. N., & Maratsos, M. P. (1977). Early comprehension of mental verbs: Think and know. *Child Development*, **48**, 1743–1747.

Johnson, C. N., & Wellman, H. M. (1982). Children's developing conceptions of the mind and brain. *Child Development*, **53**, 222–234.

Limber, J. (1973). The genesis of complex sentences. In T. E. Moore (Ed.), *Cognitive development and the acquisition of language.* New York: Academic.

McCormick, P. (1994). *Children's understanding of mind: A case for cultural diversity.* Unpublished doctoral dissertation, University of Toronto (Ontario Institute for Studies in Education).

Meichenbaum, D., & Biemiller, A. (1992). In search of student expertise in the classroom: A metacognitive analysis. In M. Pressley, K. Harris, & J. Guthrie (Eds.), *Promoting academic competence and literacy: Cognitive research and instructional innovation.* New York: Academic.

Moore, C., Bryant, D., & Furrow, D. (1989). Mental terms and the development of certainty. *Child Development,* **60,** 167–171.

Olson, D. R. (1994). *The world on paper.* Cambridge: Cambridge University Press.

Olson, D. R., & Astington, J. W. (1993). Thinking about thinking: Learning how to take statements and hold beliefs. *Educational Psychologist,* **28,** 7–23.

Perner, J., & Wimmer, H. (1985). "John thinks that Mary thinks that . . .": Attribution of second-order beliefs by 5- to 10-year-old children. *Journal of Experimental Child Psychology,* **39,** 437–471.

Shatz, M., Wellman, H. M., & Silber, S. (1983). The acquisition of mental verbs: A systematic investigation of the first reference to mental state. *Cognition,* **14,** 301–321.

Snell, B. (1982). *The discovery of the mind in Greek philosophy and literature* (T. G. Rosenmeyer, Trans.). New York: Dover. (Original work published in German in 1948)

Vygotsky, L. S. (1962). *Thought and language* (E. Hanfmann & G. Vakar, Trans.). Cambridge, MA: MIT Press. (Original work published in Russian in 1931)

CONTRIBUTORS

John H. Flavell (Ph.D. 1955, Clark University) is the Anne T. and Robert M. Bass Professor in the School of Humanities at Stanford University. His research has focused on various aspects of cognitive development, especially children's developing knowledge about the mind. He is past president of the Society for Research in Child Development and a recipient of the American Psychological Association Distinguished Scientific Contribution Award.

Frances L. Green (M.S. 1968, Specialist's Certification in School Psychological Services 1971, Ferkauf Graduate School of Humanities and Social Sciences, Yeshiva University) has been conducting research with John and Eleanor Flavell since 1977. Her research interests focus on developmental psychology in general and children's understanding of the mind in particular.

Eleanor R. Flavell (B.S. 1951, University of Maryland) has been a research assistant, working with John Flavell and Frances Green, at Stanford University since 1977.

Paul L. Harris (D.Phil. 1971, Oxford University) is university lecturer in psychology at Oxford University and a fellow of St. John's College. His interests include the development of emotion and imagination. He is the author of *Children and Emotion* (1989).

Janet Wilde Astington (Ph.D. 1985, University of Toronto, OISE) is associate professor of education at the Institute of Child Study, University of Toronto. Her research focuses on children's developing theories of mind. She is the author of *The Child's Discovery of the Mind* (1993).

STATEMENT OF EDITORIAL POLICY

The *Monographs* series is intended as an outlet for major reports of developmental research that generate authoritative new findings and use these to foster a fresh and/or better-integrated perspective on some conceptually significant issue or controversy. Submissions from programmatic research projects are particularly welcome; these may consist of individually or group-authored reports of findings from some single large-scale investigation or of a sequence of experiments centering on some particular question. Multiauthored sets of independent studies that center on the same underlying question can also be appropriate; a critical requirement in such instances is that the various authors address common issues and that the contribution arising from the set as a whole be both unique and substantial. In essence, irrespective of how it may be framed, any work that contributes significant data and/or extends developmental thinking will be taken under editorial consideration.

Submissions should contain a minimum of 80 manuscript pages (including tables and references); the upper limit of 150–175 pages is much more flexible (please submit four copies; a copy of every submission and associated correspondence is deposited eventually in the archives of the SRCD). Neither membership in the Society for Research in Child Development nor affiliation with the academic discipline of psychology are relevant; the significance of the work in extending developmental theory and in contributing new empirical information is by far the most crucial consideration. Because the aim of the series is not only to advance knowledge on specialized topics but also to enhance cross-fertilization among disciplines or subfields, it is important that the links between the specific issues under study and larger questions relating to developmental processes emerge as clearly to the general reader as to specialists on the given topic.

Potential authors who may be unsure whether the manuscript they are planning would make an appropriate submission are invited to draft an outline of what they propose and send it to the Editor for assessment. This mechanism, as well as a more detailed description of all editorial policies, evaluation processes, and format requirements, is given in the "Guidelines for the Preparation of *Monographs* Submissions," which can be obtained by writing to the Editor, Rachel K. Clifton, Department of Psychology, University of Massachusetts, Amherst, MA 01003.